THE DEVELOPMENT OF PERSONAL CONSTRUCT PSYCHOLOGY

by
Robert A. Neimeyer

Foreword by
Don Bannister

University of Nebraska Press
Lincoln and London

Copyright 1985 by the
University of Nebraska Press
All rights reserved
Manufactured in the
United States of America
The paper in this book
meets the guidelines for
permanence and durability
of the Committee on
Production Guidelines for
Book Longevity of the
Council on Library Resources.

Library of Congress Cataloging
in Publication Data

Neimeyer, Robert A., 1954–
The development of
personal construct psychology.

Bibliography: p.
Includes index.
1. Personal construct theory.
2. Personal construct theory—United States.
3. Personal construct theory—Great Britain. I. Title.
BF698.9.P47N45 1985
155.2   84-17367
ISBN 0-8032-3308-6 (alk. paper)

CONTENTS

FIGURES

Originating in 1955 with the publication of George Kelly's *Psychology of Personal Constructs*, construct theory represents an innovative and fast-growing "cognitive" approach to psychological research and practice. *The Development of Personal Construct Psychology* draws on methods developed in the sociology of science to provide a detailed socio-historical study of this subdiscipline—the only study of its kind to examine the growth of a psychological specialty.

Starting with Kelly's pioneering work, Robert A. Neimeyer traces the development of the "theory group" aligned with Kelly's position from its beginnings in the almost solitary work of its founder to the multinational network of social scientists currently applying construct theory to problems in clinical, personality, social, and developmental psychology, and even to fields as diverse as cultural anthropology and urban design. After chronicling the social history of the field through an investigation of the published output and social communication patterns of its adherents, Neimeyer appraises construct theory's current status as a discipline and discusses its problems and prospects in light of its social and intellectual history.

Exemplifying the concerns and techniques of the sociology of science, this study applies Nicholas Mullins's model for the development of scientific disciplines—a model that has been successfully applied to fields ranging from symbolic interactionism to molecular biology. The tools for this analysis include an evaluation of the style and volume of works published in the discipline over its first quarter century, the compilation of professional biographies of scores of theory group members to examine their collegial and apprenticeship ties to one another, and the construction of coauthorship maps that suggest the cohesiveness of the group's communication structure and level of disciplinary maturity.

An assistant professor of psychology at Memphis State University, Robert A. Neimeyer is the author of over forty articles and books in such areas as depression, cognitive therapy, and the development of personal relationships, many of which draw on personal construct concepts and methods.

TABLES

FOREWORD

Science has its own particular snobbery whereby it represents itself as a unique march to Truth, characterized by the special capacity of scientists to purify their logic. In psychology this snobbery takes the form of offering contrasting explanations of the behavior of scientists-psychologists on the one hand and their subject matter—ordinary mortals—on the other. Thus, psychologists present themselves as thoughtful theorizers, bold experimenters, and objective observers, whereas their subject matter—the rest of humankind—is depicted as a flotsam, pushed hither and yon by the vagaries of genetics or unconscious infantile conflicts, or environmental stimuli.

George Kelly, in inventing personal construct theory, set out to depict all persons as scientists or, for that matter, all scientists as persons. He strove to build a reflexive theory; a theory that would account for its own creation and its creator and use one language only to describe all human endeavor and confusion. By arguing that our desire to understand and anticipate is at the center of our human nature, Kelly judged science to be only a Sunday-best version of an everyday activity.

It is therefore singularly fitting that personal construct theory should be made the subject of sociohistorical analysis, as in this book. The theory declares itself to be a fallible invention of its time and place, and nothing would have pleased George Kelly more than to see his work and its development thus inspected. He wanted it to be regarded as one part of that very human mixture of creative guesswork and cooperative venturing that we formally call *science* and informally call *living*.

The book is itself reflexive in that, while arguing that science has a sociology, it recognizes that sociology has a sociology. Thus the study has both micro and macro boundaries. It tells the story of the development of personal construct theory at a variety of levels, but there are also levels of person-discipline interaction in the individual lives of its dramatis personae that are inevitably unexplored. Equally, there are pervasive social and political contexts and movements within which psychology is currently developing that are left outside the compass of this book. Yet, within its acknowledged boundaries this volume describes that interplay of person, institution, and argument that make up the drama out of which psychology evolves. It explores the family life of science, in general, and one important development in psychology, in particular. It brings to light intriguing paradoxes—the way in which the ideological grip of behaviorism in the 1950s and '60s both inhibited academic interest in personal construct theory ideas and, at the same time, stimulated a younger generation of psychologists to see construct theory as a radical form of humanistic protest. In tracking the worldwide diffusion of personal construct theory, Neimeyer's work illustrates national differences in the way in which academic intellectual life is organized in America and Britain. Above all, it records and acknowledges the social liveliness of ideas.

The book well serves two related purposes. It offers all who are concerned with the development of science (and that should include many more than just scientists) a study that exemplifies the styles and social bases of that development. Equally, it adds to the professional self-awareness of those who are concerned with the development of personal construct theory. It demonstrates that sociohistorical analyses can help to elaborate the scientific endeavors they set out to comment upon.

DON BANNISTER

ACKNOWLEDGMENTS

Undertaking a project of this nature virtually ensures that one will become indebted to many people. In a general but very important sense, I am indebted to three of my former instructors: Sanford Sussell, Gregor Sebba, and R. Taylor Scott. Although they may be unaware of my completion of this project, each of them in his own way helped give me the courage to ask big questions. I owe a more immediate debt of gratitude to Mike Acree, Bill Arnold, and Monte Page, all of whom made me aware of the importance of history and theory in psychology, and who by their personal examples encouraged me to pursue a project close to my heart even at the risk of its being unconventional. Similarly, I wish to express my appreciation to Don Bannister, Ray Holland, Miller Mair, Dorothy Rowe, Han Bonarius, Fay Fransella, and my brother Greg Neimeyer, all active participants in the theory whose social history I have attempted to set down. Along with the many others who granted me interviews, they breathed life into the research by sharing with me the stories of their own personal encounters with construct theory and construct theorists.

Seth Krieger and Franz Epting deserve particular mention, the former for having introduced me to the theory that has become so much a part of my life, the latter for having allowed me to work beside him as a genuine colleague during the years of my apprenticeship at the University of Florida. I owe a special debt to Al Landfield, my adviser during my graduate training at the University of Nebraska–Lincoln. Through his faith in me, his gentle criticism, and his almost fatherly concern, he encouraged me to reach beyond my specialty of clinical psychology to place in broader perspective the movement of which I was a part. Most of all, I appreciate his giving me that most precious form of guidance—the freedom to pursue my own interests.

Finally, I wish to thank Kathy Story, whose constant love, support, and understanding have made it all worthwhile.

1

INTRODUCTION

I hope that personal construct theory is, or can become great. As I see it, this will come about if it applies to itself all the resources of socio-psychological analysis in deep-going self-criticism, the only way of moving beyond "ambiguities." (Ray Holland, 1981, p. 28)

A. Overview of the Project

Writing an *intellectual* history of a discipline can serve many functions. At its best, such writing can offer a critical account of the flow of ideas characterizing the field at various points in its development, tracing its progress from its historical sources, recounting its convergence with other streams of thought, and mapping its present currents and directions. At its worst, such writing can degenerate into the historically naive measurement of previous theorizing against the standard of contemporary knowledge, or the self-congratulatory implication that the current discipline represents the fruition of all earlier labors, it remaining for future workers simply to fill in the outlines of the essentially "correct" theoretical framework bequeathed by the present.

Writing a *sociological*, as distinct from an intellectual, history of a discipline can serve other, equally critical ends. If one accepts the premise that all communicable knowledge arises within a social context, then it follows that an examination of that context can elucidate social factors that condition or shape the knowledge it produces. Because any discipline provides a framework that both extends and restricts the intellectual vision of its adherents, a sociopsychological analysis can suggest *limitations* in its theorizing that derive in part from its particular social history.

The present work represents my effort to explicate certain aspects of the sociohistorical development of George Kelly's (1955) personal construct theory (PCT). As a theory of personality and clinical psychology, PCT is founded on the assumption that individuals function as *personal scientists*, attempting to devise conceptual templates (personal constructs) that permit them to interpret, anticipate, and appropriately respond to the events with which they are confronted. By emphasizing as he did the capacity of persons to substantially construct the meanings of their lives, and to refine these meanings in light of subsequent experience, Kelly (1955) departed from both the environmental determinism of radical behaviorist formulations and the intrapsychic determinism of classical psychoanalysis. Yet, despite his humanistic leanings, he did not align himself with philosophically sympathetic "third force" psychologies (Holland, 1970), in part because he was suspicious of their phenomenalism and antiempirical stance. Instead, Kelly drafted a new kind of psychological theory: one focusing on the structure and function of the individual's construing activity, on the way in which *systems* of personal constructs are organized and are subject to change over time. Because he was concerned that PCT be tested, revised, and applied by other psychologists, he also provided a flexible psychometric technique, the Role Construct Repertory Grid, or Repgrid, by means of which the structural features of construct systems could be assessed (Fransella & Bannister, 1977).

Over the past thirty years PCT has contributed to considerable research in personality, social, and clinical psychology, fostering extensive study of such topics as cognitive complexity and schizophrenic thought disorder.[1] Despite its origin as an American theory, it has gained adherents throughout the English-speaking world, particularly in Great Britain, where it has become more visible than in the United States. The broad academic base that PCT has enjoyed, coupled with the internationality of its following, makes its development especially interesting to trace. Such an analysis seems particularly appropriate at the present historical moment. As M. J. Mulkay (1976) notes, the evolution of scientific disciplines is seldom as straightforward as is commonly believed. Rather, such development usually proceeds irregularly and necessarily involves periodic reappraisals and redefinitions. I believe that PCT is in the midst of such a period of reappraisal, as the critical and reflective tone of recent construct theoretical work suggests (c.f. Holland, 1981; McCoy, 1977; Radley, 1977; Rathod, 1981; Stefan, 1977; Stringer, 1979; Tyler, 1981). Moreover, I believe, as does R. Holland (1981, p. 25), that "it is possible for personal construct theory to 'know itself' [and thereby establish the directions in which it must next move] by the application to it of a developed form of the sociology of knowledge." In the following chapters I will attempt to take a step toward the realization of this goal.

My major conceptual tool for studying PCT's emergence will be N. C. Mullins's (1973) model for the development of scientific disciplines. In section B of this introduction, I explicate the four stages of disciplinary progress outlined by the model, and discuss their related social and intellectual properties. In Chapter 2 I begin the study by examining the "birth" of Kelly's theory of personality, and the senses in which it embodied certain themes that were rooted in the personal and social contexts of its author's life. Chapter 3 broadens the inquiry to a consideration of the social-structural progress made by PCT in the United States, as reflected in the establishment of research and training centers in the theory, the type and quantity of its published output, and the consolidation of coauthorship links among its adherents. Chapters 4 and 5 are structured similarly, treating the development of PCT in Great Britain and other countries, respectively. Chapter 6 further enlarges this picture by examining international trends in the theory's development that transcend those evident in particular nations. In Chapter 7, I apply Mullins's (1973) model to the "raw data" of the previous chapters in order to describe PCT's sociohistorical development and assess its current degree of maturity as a scientific discipline. Finally, in Chapter 8 I conclude with a discussion of several focal issues (e.g., PCT's "intellectual isolationism," the possibility of forming an international organization) that represent both problems and prospects for contemporary construct theorists.

Before moving forward with this analysis, I need to insert a cautionary note. My attempt at a sociohistorical description and critique admittedly is affected not only by my position as a *clinical psychol-*

ogist—a specialization that, as Holland (1979) notes, virtually disqualifies me from knowing "finely and sensitively" the field of sociology of science—but also because I am a *construct theorist*. I am forced at the outset to acknowledge that in my own outlook I have taken up, often at unconscious levels, precisely those assumptions and prejudices that most severely limit the meaningful revision of PCT to approximate a more adequate theory of human functioning. Furthermore, although my "insider" status gave me certain initial impressions concerning the sociology of the theory, such knowledge was acquired while I was "a comparatively uncritical participant and [therefore] is a social construct of doubtful validity" (Mulkay, 1976, p. 209). I have tried to deal with the limitations that my own social position imposes on this investigation by clearly labeling my own biases and opinions when I am aware of their intruding into my discussion and, as Mulkay (1976, p. 207) suggests, utilizing "multiple indicators" of the discipline's development. Obviously, such precautionary measures cannot eliminate all traces of "subjectivity" from what follows, but I hope that they will assure that some of the *advantages* of my insider status (e.g., acquaintance with the "content" of personal construct theory and research) can be retained while the disadvantages are minimized.

B. Mullins's Model for the Development of Scientific Disciplines

In recent years, sociologists have attempted to investigate empirically the growth of those knowledge systems granted pre-eminence in our time—the disciplines and specialties of science (Becker, 1981). In applying to the study of science the principles of their discipline, sociologists have de-emphasized the strictly historical recounting of "the internal development of knowledge within given fields of inquiry," and instead "have tended to concentrate on the social processes associated with the activities of scientists" (Lemaine, MacLeod, Mulkay & Weingart, 1976, p. 1). Such studies typically attempt to account for developments within a given discipline by analyzing various aspects of its social functioning: features of its communication structure, its institutional context, its published literature, its mechanisms for scientific recognition and reward, and so on. Perhaps because of the important contribution made by the natural sciences to our political, economic, and intellectual life, the bulk of this work has focused upon the evolution of "hard" science, rather than "human" science disciplines (c.f.

Mulkay, 1979). Recently, however, Mullins (1972, 1973) has expounded a general model of disciplinary development that has proven applicable to fields as diverse as molecular biology and sociology's symbolic interactionism. It is Mullins's model, outlined below, that I have applied to the growth of personal construct psychology.

Essentially, Mullins's model traces the progress of the nascent "theory group" (i.e., a coherent group of scientists sharing a common theoretical orientation and interest in a related set of problems) as it gradually differentiates from its parent discipline and eventually matures to become a specialty in its own right. The basic feature of this process is the changing *pattern* of *communication* within the emerging group. Connections between members of a theory group, like those between scientists in the general scientific communication structure, consist of four types of professional/social relationships:

(1) *communication*, serious discussion about ongoing research;
(2) *coauthorship*, a more intimate form of association in which two or more scientists jointly publish a theoretical, practical or research contribution;
(3) *apprenticeship*, the training of a student by his or her teacher;
(4) *colleagueship*, two scientists working at the same institution (Mullins, 1973, p. 19).

As a theory group congeals, less formal communication ties (often with persons outside the scientist's focal area of interest) are augmented by closer coauthor, apprentice, and colleague relations among group members. Of course, any *given* scientist will continue to form and break many such ties during the course of her or his research career. But the degree of cohesion in the communication structure linking group members as an aggregate will suggest the amount of social structural progress made by the theory group. Additionally, Mullins holds that certain specifiable intellectual developments accompany the social communicative changes undergone by the emerging group. For the sake of conceptual clarity, he segments this continual evolutionary process into the following four stages.

Normal Stage. Like T. Kuhn (1970), Mullins characterizes a scientific discipline in the normal stage as occupied with "bit and piece puzzle solving." The scientific literature in the particular area is produced by isolated researchers at scattered institutions. It displays a relatively low degree of organization, since the researchers involved lack the stable social relationships—durable student, coauthor, and colleague ties—that would produce a coordinated effort toward exploring common problems. Nonetheless, the seeds of a new research area may exist in the closely related work of scientists at different places, who often may be unaware of similar work proceeding elsewhere (Lemaine et al., 1976, p. 5). This stage ends when an exciting intellectual product (e.g., empirical, theoretical, or critical work) catalyzes theory group development by attracting several other researchers. Seldom is the emerging orientation recognized immediately by the parent discipline as an important departure or major challenge, although it may be seen as such in historical hindsight.

Network Stage. The network stage begins when scientists who have gathered around an important new discovery, idea, or criticism begin to conduct discussions of their work among themselves, rather than with workers whose major interests lie elsewhere. This produces a local "thickening" of the scientific communication structure (Griffith & Mullins, 1972) that is increased as group members begin to attract a few students and to recruit one another as colleagues. As consensus about the shared aims of the group begins to develop, agreements on the style and direction of future research are reached and often are codified in a *program statement* by the group's *intellectual leader.* Typically, a *training center* and a *research center* develop during this stage, when two or more individuals at a single location begin teaching and conducting research in the new style. By and large, however, the relations among group members remain informal, and the size of the total group seldom numbers over forty before the next stage of development is attained. Mullins estimates that theory groups ordinarily remain in the network stage four to fourteen years, depending upon the degree to which factors in their parent discipline and the society at large favor their further development.

Cluster Stage. The publication of work resulting from consensus often ushers in the cluster stage. The appearance of intellectual successes attracts other scientists, and constellations of colleagues and students begin to form around intellectual leaders at one or more research centers. As these local groupings grow to sufficient size to achieve stable "cluster" status (minimally seven persons, at least three of whom have completed training), apprentice and colleague relationships continue to displace the informal relations characteristic of earlier stages. Communication becomes even more ingrown. Group members' contacts with professionals outside the cluster are largely with others having similar interests, and the burgeoning research literature by the theory group contains fewer citations to work generated from other perspectives. Close collaboration between group members leads to more widespread coauthorship, a factor that further increases the theoretical consistency of the research front.[2]

As the group becomes more vigorous, it is crucial that one or more persons assume a position of *social leadership*, arranging for the meetings, jobs, and publications needed to maintain the group through its period of clusterhood. Often this is accomplished by an intellectual leader, but this need not be the case. Partly as a result of these social/organizational efforts, the theory group becomes more visible to the parent discipline, and outside critical work related to the group's emphasis begins to appear. This reaction establishes the new group as either *elite* or *revolutionary* (Griffith & Mullins, 1972). The elite group enjoys the respect of the parent discipline, and its reformulations are regarded as significant contributions to scientific knowledge. The revolutionary group, on the other hand, is regarded as either dangerous or foolish in its rejection of accepted theorizing. It may be "encapsulated" by the larger discipline until it fades away, successfully overthrows the status quo, or becomes the establishment view for another specialty or discipline. The length of time the theory group spends in the cluster phase depends partly upon its elite or revolutionary status, since successful students and colleagues will be hired away from the former more quickly than from the latter. Generally, however, Mullins estimates that clusterhood usually last four to eight years.

Specialty Stage. Ironically, as the successful cluster grows in visibility and importance in the eyes of the parent discipline, its stability is increasingly jeopardized by the hiring efforts of groups at competing institutions. This trend toward eventual dissolution is given internal impetus by the exigencies of the academic community, where most training and research centers are situated, since few universities devoted to broad-based education can afford for long the homogeneity of research interest characteristic of the active cluster. As the personal ties of the earlier phase become weakened through attrition of its members, the theory group gradually enters the specialty stage. During this final stage of social structural development, the primary task of the group is to institutionalize the work that has been done. Not surprisingly, the means by which elite and revolutionary groups accomplish this task differ in some respects. The elite specialty, existing in a relatively friend-ly intellectual environment, establishes communication ties easily and takes over established journals and positions in order to create space for its members within the larger professional community. The revolution-ary group, on the other hand, having more adversarial relations with the parent discipline, is forced to establish new positions and publication outlets if it is to mature to specialty status. In the case of the latter group, this transition may be slowed by the group members themselves, who may be reluctant to relinquish the strong in-group feeling engendered by their longer history as a cluster and their common survival in the face of opposition to their development. Specialty-level development in both groups, however, may depend on the development of a new kind of social organizational leader, one more willing to become bureaucra-tized.

As the once tightly-linked network of collaborators begins to dis-perse, social communication patterns begin once again to assume the informal pattern of normal science. Scattered network thickenings per-sist for a time, but these gradually disintegrate as members' involve-ments continue to diversify. The total intellectual output of the group may continue to grow early in the specialty stage. The character of this work differs, however, from the ground-breaking successes of the net-work and cluster periods. Secondary materials (e.g., edited volumes, review articles, textbooks) appear in order to preserve the distinctiveness of the position and, at the same time, grant others some familiarity with its basic tenets. Despite these efforts, the intellectual production of the group continues to differentiate, since it has become too large to be held to a dogmatic line by "the immediate mechanisms of conversations and lectures" (Mullins, 1973, p. 203). Parts of the group may begin to drift away as members begin to integrate the teachings of the theory group with their own unique intellectual biographies. Eventually, all that re-mains of the specialty is "a name, sometimes a longing for the good old days of clusterhood, and occasionally, a conscious history" (Mullins, 1973, p. 25).

Mullins is careful to point out that there is nothing inevitable about a theory group's progression through the stages from normal sci-ence to specialty. In fact, the failure to negotiate one or more of its essential hurdles is the most likely outcome (Mullins, 1973, p. 106). Nonetheless, Mullins unflinchingly measures a group's success in terms of its attainment of specialty status, that is, its impact upon the parent discipline:

> How do we distinguish successful groups from failures? One possibility is to define as a failure every potential group of scientists that does not develop the characteristics noted previously [e.g., research and training centers, intellectual materials, an important theoretical break from parent discipline]. If we take this approach, however, virtually every development in every time period is ultimately unsuccessful. This is a drastic but honest conclusion. Most scientists and most potential developments do *not* contribute to changing the course of science. (Mullins, 1973, p. 27)

In many of the following chapters, I will be applying aspects of Mullins's basic model to study features of the development of personal construct psychology as a theory group. Before undertaking this sociohistorical task, however, I will explore briefly the *prehistory* of PCT in the strata of George Kelly's life before his emergence as a major personality theorist.

2

THE BIRTH OF PERSONAL CONSTRUCT THEORY

Before studying personal construct theory's public development, it may be helpful to take a backward glance over that period in Kelly's life when the theory was gestating, so to speak, before its presentation to the psychological community in 1955. A close scrutiny of the life and work of any personality theorists could trace in detail those biographical themes and events that shaped the style and content of their psychological formulations. [1] My aim here is more limited; the brief and selective treatment of George Kelly's life that follows is intended to convey only a sense of how his theory was formulated and to illustrate the way in which it came to embody certain aspects of Kelly's own self-understanding.

A suitable place to begin such a task is with Kelly's childhood. As J. Rychlak (1973) describes, Kelly was born in 1905, the only child of farming parents near Perth, Kansas. The rural isolation of the tiny farming community cultivated in its inhabitants a resourcefulness and sense of self-reliance that might have been less of a requisite for survival in a more populous social environment. Don Bannister's recollection of his own visit to Kelly's home town suggests the sort of impact that growing up in such a context might have had on the development of personal construct theory:

I took a 200-mile detour to visit Perth, Kansas, and I'm not actually sure I visited it. Because the signpost said, "Perth 7 miles." So I set the odometer on the car and I was in the middle of this vast kind of billiard table. And I passed a cemetery that had quite a few gravestones in it, so there must have been something there at some time, but it had long gone. There was a farm in the distance, and I passed about four more en route. But in England we just never see that amount of space with nothing much in it. . . . Somebody had been telling me about Sartre, and they were telling me he grew up in Paris, and he looked out over the vast view of roofs, and houses, and tenements, and people crowded in piles. And I did suddenly get a sense of contrast, that, stuck out there on a farm in Kansas, if you didn't *imagine* something, then there wouldn't be much there. You'd have to make something out of it. . . . Miller Mair said somewhere that Kelly got the wrong model [for his theory]. The actual model is "man-the-pioneer" [in contrast to Kelly's (1955) "man-the-scientist" metaphor]. And that related to Kelly's personal life, that he came from pioneering stock. He grew up on the kind of Kansas farm where you invent everything you need. And he carried that over. (Bannister, 1979, personal communication)

Bannister acknowledges here the influence that Kelly's boyhood experience on the plains may have had upon the content of the personality theory he later authored. Specifically, he implies that Kelly's later emphasis on the capacity of persons to invent or create the meaning of their lives reflects the premium that his early environment must have placed on imagination and inventiveness. Moreover, Kelly's pioneering background—he and his parents literally were among the last "homesteaders" on the American frontier—undoubtedly predisposed him to conceptualize human behavior in terms of an "exploration" or "quest," in terms that J. M. M. Mair believes echo the tone of much of Kelly's work.

The kind of venture which seems to me to assume a central place in personal construct psychology is not of the "big game hunting" or "conquering Everest" variety. It is something both more homey and more audacious. What Kelly seems to be advocating is something like "life on the frontier"—living on the frontiers of your experience rather than within cosily settled conventions or as a more-or-less willing victim of the demands of tradition. You can almost hear the "wagon trains moving westward," seeking new pastures and more space for living, as you read Kelly's writings. (Mair, 1977a, p. 268)

By maintaining that Kelly's social context "influenced" or "shaped" his theorizing, I do not mean to imply that it *caused* him to theorize as he did, in any mechanistic or unidirectional sense of the word. Rather, I mean to suggest that his context was important in establishing the fund of experience upon which he could draw in creatively formulating his theory. I am aware that this interpretation is more consonant with my own construct-theoretical/phenomenological biases (Merleau-Ponty, 1976) than it is with the more reductionist or deterministic programs within the sociology of knowledge (e.g., Bloor, 1976). However, recent sociologists of science have begun to espouse a less "casual" program for their discipline, one based less on an artificial and highly idealized conception of the goals of science. Speaking from this more humanistic perspective, E. Millstone remarks, "We grow out of our past, we take the given conditions and go beyond them, we transcend or 'cut across' the given situation. Our thoughts, beliefs, knowledge and actions are not reducible to the social and material conditions which occasion them" (1978, p. 113).

While more humanistic observers like Millstone reject the proposition that early social factors inexorably determine the content of a theorist's later work, neither do they embrace the equally untenable position that a theorist's life experiences play no part in his or her theorizing. Even construct theorists acknowledge that a "total" psychological theory must be "reflexive," i.e., must be capable of interpreting the experience of its author, if it is to avoid self-contradiction (Oliver & Landfield, 1962). M. Polanyi (1958) argues more broadly that even the most purely "scientific" knowledge claim ultimately carries a "personal coefficient." But it is necessary to recognize that the central themes that inform any theory of personality—themes that derive in part from the author's unique social and biographical context—obscure some aspects of its subject matter while highlighting others. In fact, it is just this capacity of constructs (whether personal or theoretical) to "channelize" awareness that Kelly used as the cornerstone for his theorizing (Kelly, 1955).

If this is granted, then it becomes important to ask what aspects of human experience Kelly's background may have led him to treat less adequately, what may lie outside the "focus of convenience" of his theory, to use Kelly's own (1955) terminology. As Bannister and Mair rightly remarked, PCT lends itself to conceptualizing the creative, self-reliant, exploratory actions of individuals. But its very stress upon individualism, inventiveness, and humanity's "noble struggle"[2] necessarily leads the theory to deemphasize complex social phenomena, especially those that are based on clear exploitation or conflict (Holland, 1977).

The self-reliance of Kelly's childhood seems to be reflected in the *form* of his theorizing as well as its *content*. This is especially apparent in Kelly's failure to find intellectual support in compatible phenomenological and existential thinkers, while at the same time reinventing a homespun version of their philosophy for inclusion in his own theory. It seems less likely that Kelly was purposely misinterpreting such work in order to differentiate it from his own, than that he simply had little firsthand awareness of such kindred traditions.[3] This more benign interpretation is supported by Kelly's own "bootstrap" educational history, during which he earned a patchwork of degrees in physics, mathematics, and education before studying psychology—for a single year— and completing his Ph.D. at Iowa State University in 1931.

In the fall of that year, Kelly joined the faculty of Fort Hays Kansas State College.[4] The pressing social need for practical psychological interventions, especially in the school systems, soon diverted him from his nascent interest in experimentation on perception (c.f. Kelly, 1933). This transition from the laboratory to the consulting room proved decisive for Kelly's thought, for it forced him to grapple with the clinical realities that were to form the grounding for his later, more abstract theorizing.

Although Kelly's writings during his thirteen-year period at Hays largely concerned the practical treatment innovations he introduced as director of the psychology clinic, it is possible to discern in them the seeds of ideas that would later occupy important positions in *The Psychology of Personal Constructs* (1955). For example, it is noteworthy, in light of allegations that PCT represents an "intellectual" or "cognitive" approach to psychotherapy (c.f. Rogers, 1956), that Kelly (1938, pp. 95–96) remarked, "Personality disorders are usually best treated by some form of *rational* therapy. Rational therapy consists of showing the patient how to "think through" his difficulty" (Kelly's italics). This emphasis on the client's ability to "reconstrue" life in new, more adaptive ways persists in his later writings, although by 1955 Kelly had tempered the "cognitive" flavor of his earlier therapeutic style, frequently making use of such evocative techniques as role-playing (R. A. Neimeyer, 1980).

Even in his early years as a therapist, Kelly (1938) was attempting to develop a therapy that offered an alternative to the then-dominant medical model. He envisioned the task of therapy as an "educative" one, proceeding by a series of "discoveries" on the part of the patient. To facilitate this process, he developed an elaborate form for the diagnostic interview, with questions concentrating on topics that had proven to be "turning points" in the hundreds of cases he had researched (e.g., self-description, suicide ideation, family/marital discord, religion, sexuality). Elsewhere he anticipated the idiographic structure of the Role Construct Repertory Test (Kelly, 1955, chaps. 5, 6) in speaking of the need for "devices . . . which give character and pattern to individual case studies" (Kelly, 1940, p. 576). Along with a student, Kelly also experimented with a novel kind of projective testing "constructed from the presupposition that people identify themselves with strong characters in stories they read" (Bishop & Kelly, 1942, p. 599). The technique consisted of presenting the respondent with a series of story plots and requiring that he or she select the "solution" to the "conflict" represented in the story. The emphasis in this technique on the "as if" identification with a hypothetical character foreshadowed his later therapeutic practice of writing a carefully designed "character sketch" of an imaginary personality, which the client then would be instructed to enact in his or her everyday life for a time-limited period (Kelly, 1955, chaps. 7, 8). Kelly assumed that this playful identification with a different outlook on life could enable the client to recognize that even the most familiar of events could appear utterly transformed if only they were construed differently. In fact, Kelly was experimenting with a standardized form of "role therapy" even at this early stage of his thinking (Robinson & Kelly, 1942), a decade before he integrated it into a personal construct approach to clinical practice.

These prewar publications (as well as the numerous unpublished procedure manuals written for the Hays clinic) reveal Kelly as clinically systematic, often innovative, but always eminently practical. With the advent of World War II and his placement in the Aviation Psychology Branch of the U.S. Navy, he was forced to table these strictly diagnostic and therapeutic interests and turn his attention instead to the study of "war weariness" among pilots, instrument panel design, and other pressing problems of applied psychology (e.g., Kelly, 1945a; 1945b; 1945c). Although the war may have interrupted the development of his earlier pursuits, it also may have given him his first experience with interdisciplinary collaboration, which he was later to champion in his role as one of the founding fathers of clinical psychology.

Following the war, Kelly accepted a placement briefly at the University of Maryland and in 1946 was appointed professor and director of clinical psychology at Ohio State University, where he continued to teach until 1965. His early postwar writings followed his prewar pattern of concern for practical issues (e.g., Kelly, 1946). However, as OSU achieved national prominence as a training center for clinical psychologists, he became more engaged in professional concerns (eventually serving as president of both the consulting and the clinical divisions of the American Psychological Association). At the same time, he became increasingly oriented to developing psychological theory as well as praxis.

By the late 1940s, Kelly began reading more theoretical manuscripts to his students, and by 1951 the rudiments of personal construct psychology were sufficiently well formed for Kelly to present a paper on the topic to a gathering of professionals in Houston, Texas (Kelly, 1951). Four years later, in the preface to his magnum opus, Kelly traced his progress in committing to paper the theoretical stance that had been implicit in his earlier work:

> This book started out twenty years ago as a handbook of clinical procedures. It was designed for the writer's students and used as a guide in the clinic of which he was the director. . . . From this beginning the handbook was supposed to develop gradually into something which might have wider use. But, time after time, the writing bogged down in a morass of tedious little maxims. It was no good—this business of trying to tell the reader merely *how* to deal with clinical problems; the *why* kept insistently rearing its puzzling head.
>
> So we started to write about the *whys*. It was encouraging to find words trickling out behind the typewriter keys again. Yet no sooner had we started than something strange began to happen; or rather, we discovered that something unsuspected had already happened. It turned out to be this: in the years of relatively isolated clinical practice we had wandered far off the beaten paths of psychology, much farther than we had ever suspected.
>
> And now how far afield were we? Or, what was more important, could our readers ever find us? Obviously we had been making many basic assumptions implicitly—taking for granted our somewhat unusual convictions. Unless we now were able to become explicit about such matters could we ever hope to say sensible things to anybody about the *whys* of clinical practice? It seemed not.
>
> We backed off and started again, this time at the level of system building. It was a half-and-half job; half invention of coherent assumptions which

would sustain a broad field of inquiry, and half articulation of convictions we had already been taking for granted. (Kelly, 1955, pp. ix–x)

The result, in the words of Jerome Bruner (1956), was received as "a genuine new departure and spirited contribution to the psychology of personality," one that would continue to gain momentum thirty years later.

3

PERSONAL CONSTRUCT THEORY IN THE UNITED STATES

A. American Research and Training Centers

After Kelly's articulation of the tenets of PCT in 1955, the crucial question for the fledgling theory became whether or not it could attract enough adherents to remain viable. If it were to be more than a stillborn theoretical statement, it needed to be taken up by others who would extend, refine, test, and apply Kelly's initial conceptualization. This was crucial, because "promising ideas in a field will not develop without serious follow-through in terms of student training and group development" (Mullins, 1973, p. 252). PCT was successful in attracting such a "theory group." In this chapter I will study the evolving institutional structure of this group in the United States and its impact upon the growth of the theory.

According to Mullins (1973, pp. 12–13), an identifiable theory group can be said to have formed when a small, coherent group of scientists develops, who work on a set of related problems of mutual interest, and find that their formulations differ from those of their parent discipline and are similar to those of each other.[1] By the mid-1950s, such a group had coalesced within PCT, concentrating upon "a somewhat narrow, but clearly defined, set of related problems" chiefly pertaining to the "systematic assessment of individual differences in cognitive structure by means of repertory grid technique" (Adams-Webber, 1979, pp. xi, 19).

Of course, if one wishes to subject the development of a theory group to more than global or impressionistic analysis, some method of clearly identifying members of the group must be devised. Unfortunately, the "obvious" method of asking certain group members to identify those who fall within the "boundary" of their discipline proves to be unsatisfactory. As Mullins states,

> The perceptions of group members are neither singular nor determining of membership—not singular in that every person in a group has not been polled on group membership; not determining because, for groups in which such polling has been done, it is clear that very different "membership" lists result from: (1) differing perceptions of events, (2) tricks of memory and recall and (3) position-controlled differences in interpretation. (1973, p. 301)

The problems in this approach are further exacerbated when the theory group in question is multinational in its membership, as is PCT, since the awareness that group members may have of one another is reduced further by differences in publication outlets, possible language differences, and other cultural barriers.

My solution to this problem has been to define group membership in terms of an individual's *published contribution* to the theory. Particularly for a theory like Kelly's that has a substantial *clinical and applied*, as opposed to *academic*, base of support, the use of a membership criterion based on publication has the effect of underestimating the number of persons actively engaged in working from within the perspective. However, I believe that this criterion, though stringent, is defensible on the grounds that it 1) will reflect more accurately the membership that actually contributes to the *scientific* advancement of the theory group, and 2) will err in the direction of producing a conservative index of the group's development.

I have approached this task by first developing a *comprehensive bibliography* of all published work within construct theory—whether empirical, theoretical, or applied—and then identifying as group members those individuals who were *contributors*, i.e., who were listed as author or coauthor of at least two such reports.[2] I chose a minimum criterion of two publications, rather than one, in order to distinguish between authors who had only a passing interest in construct theory concepts or methodologies and those who had a more enduring commitment to the perspective. Using this criterion, I discovered that of the 552 different persons who had published within the theory from 1954 to 1980, 160 (29 percent) had done so at least twice. These then became the theory group members whose affiliation patterns I subjected to closer scrutiny.

In examining the social connections between contributors to PCT, I will concentrate here primarily upon the colleagueship and apprenticeship ties represented at the major training and research centers for PCT in this country. An examination of social relationships based on communication, being the most difficult to document accurately, will be attempted only in the case of those prominent construct theorists with whom I conducted personal or taped interviews. Discussion of coauthorship relations will be reserved for a separate section.

Contributors from the United States appear in table 1.[3] Construct theory's origin in clinical practice is reflected in the fact that of the sixty-eight American contributors, thirty-eight (56 percent) obtained their degrees in clinical or counseling psychology. PCT also appears to have a foothold in more traditionally academic fields, with an additional 18 percent of contributors representing developmental, social/personality, or general experimental areas. The remaining 18 percent for whom degree information was available came from a variety of disciplines, including philosophy, geography, communications, architecture, psychometrics, and social work.

Information on the institutional affiliation of each of the contributors from 1954 to 1981 also was obtained through questionnaires, interviews, and career biographies appearing in professional directories. Conceptually reorganizing these data by institution yields a depiction of the apprentice and colleague relations at each of the most influential social centers over construct theory's thirty-year history in the U.S. A brief description of each of these major centers follows.

Ohio State University, 1948–1969. The first vehicle for the dissemination of construct theoretical ideas was Kelly's evening seminar, dubbed the "Thursday Night Group," which commenced in the late 1940s at OSU. Although these meetings later evolved into formal course offerings on PCT and repertory grid technique, in the early years they were quite informal. Kelly typically would convene an interested group of students and an occasional faculty member at his home, where he would read and discuss drafts of the chapters that later would con-

Table 1
Contributors to PCT: United States

Banikiotes, P.	Howard, A. R.	Posthuma, A. B.
Betak, J. F.	Jones, R. A.	Press, A. N.
Bieri, J.	Karst, T. O.	Pyron, B.
Blackman, S.	Kelly, G. A.	Rainey, L. E.
Bodden, J. L.	Koenig, F. W.	Riedel, W. W.
Carr, J. E.	Krieger, S. R.	Rigdon, M.
Clark, R. A.	Landfield, A. W.	Rosenberg, S.
Crockett, W. H.	Leitner, L. M.	Sarbin, T. R.
Cromwell, R. G.	Lester, D.	Scott, W. A.
Danforth, N. J.	Levy, L. H.	Seaman, J. M.
Day, C. R.	Maher, B. A.	Sechrest, L.
Delia, J. G.	Mancuso, J. G.	Simmons, W. L.
Dolliver, R. H.	Merluzzi, T.	Soucar, E.
Dugan, R. D.	Miller, A. D.	Space, L. G.
Epting, F. R.	Mischel, T.	Suchman, D. I.
Francher, R. E.	Mischel, W.	Tripodi, T.
Fjeld, S. P.	Messick, S.	Tyler, F. B.
Goldstein, K. M.	Monaghan, R. R.	Vacc, N. A.
Gonyea, A. H.	Neimeyer, G. J.	Ward, W. D.
Harrison, R.	Neimeyer, R. A.	Weigel, R. G.
Handin, K.	Nidorf, L. J.	Weigel, V. M.
Higgins, K.	O'Keefe, B. J.	Wilkins, G.
Honikman, B.	Oliver, D.	Zimring, F. M.
	Phillips, W. M.	

stitute his *Psychology of Personal Constructs* (1955). In order to foster a free-flowing critique of his ideas on the part of students who otherwise felt intimidated by OSU faculty, Kelly always provided a case of cold beer at such meetings, although he himself was a teetotaler (R. L. Cromwell, 1980, personal communication).

The weekly group meetings served important social as well as intellectual functions, providing participants not only an opportunity for discussing the seminal assumptions of the new theory but also a measure of identity as "Thursday Nighters" having shared interests and direction. Of the eighteen *regular* participants at these meetings, six (J. Bieri, R. Cromwell, A. R. Howard, A. W. Landfield, L. Levy, and B. Maher) went on to become significant contributors to PCT.[4] Some of these early contributors, like James Bieri, were attracted to Kelly's thinking because they saw it as more challenging and theoretically engaging than traditional approaches to clinical psychology. Other early students, like A. W. Landfield, became involved in PCT not only because of its intellectual appeal, but also because the theory seemed to apply at a deeply personal level to their own lives. In the later years of the OSU center, the research literature generated by the group served to attract other capable students. Franz Epting, for example, was drawn to the theory indirectly by way of his initial interest in cognitive complexity, an area pioneered by Bieri a decade earlier.

Over the twenty years of its existence, the OSU center graduated a total of nineteen contributors to PCT. Many have remained active construct researchers and have moved on to establish training centers elsewhere. Others have gained recognition primarily for their work in other specialities but have continued to support the PCT theory group through their editorial and political efforts. Brendan Maher, for example, edited and published several of Kelly's important post-1955 addresses and manuscripts in book form (Maher, 1969), and Walter Mischel has worked to articulate PCT with recent cognitive research in personality (Mischel, 1981). Finally, during the 1960s the OSU center's importance was enhanced because foreign psychologists (including D. Bannister from Britain, H. Bonarius from the Netherlands, and M. Lifshitz from Israel) came to work with Kelly as students and colleagues.

Despite Kelly's ability to attract and graduate numerous students, OSU remained fragile as a training and research center for PCT, since it relied exclusively upon Kelly's energetic social and intellectual leadership. This weakness was demonstrated when OSU failed to graduate a single significant construct theorist who *began* studying after Kelly departed for Brandeis in 1966. Nevertheless, OSU's record for producing major figures in PCT remains unrivaled by any subsequent U.S. institution, clearly establishing it as the foremost American training center in the theory to date.

University of Missouri–Columbia, 1956–1972. A. W. Landfield, among the first of the Ohio State students to be deeply influenced by PCT, graduated in 1951 and assumed his first academic position at Purdue that same year. Although Purdue did not become a major research center in PCT, Landfield did cultivate an enduring friendship there with Franklin Shaw, whose work in "reconciliation theory" came to have a significant impact on Landfield's thinking about psychotherapeutic change (see Landfield & Allee, 1966). Landfield carried this developing interest in psychotherapy with him to Missouri in 1956, where he assumed directorship of the psychology clinic. Under his leadership, Missouri became a major training center in the theory, especially after his assumption of full-time academic status in 1968.

Landfield's long collaboration with Don Oliver, in the department of philosophy, helped stabilize the Missouri network. The relationship between the two men was initially based on informal communication regarding mutual interests (e.g., the construction of the self) but eventually matured into a coauthorship tie producing their classic statement on reflexivity as it pertains to personality theory (Oliver & Landfield, 1962). The stability of the Missouri group was further enhanced by the recruitment of R. H. Dolliver, one of Kelly's later students, in 1965. Unfortunately, theoretical differences between Dolliver and the others, in part concerning the importance of reflexivity (Dolliver & Woodward, 1975), limited the extent of their collaboration.

The major intellectual product of the Missouri group was an extensive program of research on the psychotherapy relationship (Landfield, 1971). This program, orchestrated by Landfield, involved numerous students (including L. Ourth, S. Fjeld, W. Danforth, G. Issacson, and two assistant professors, J. Doster and D. Varble. Kelly, Oliver, and Shaw served as consultants. Over the course of its existence, the Missouri center produced four students who have published at least twice in PCT (W. Danforth and S. Fjeld in clinical psychology and R. Weigel and V. Weigel in counseling).[5] Oliver's retirement in 1971, followed by Landfield's move to Nebraska in 1972, ended network-level activity, however, and Dolliver's lone presence at the institution failed to produce any new contributors.

Brandeis University, 1965–1967. In 1965 Kelly accepted Abraham Maslow's invitation to join the faculty at Brandeis under virtually ideal circumstances; he was given the freedom to pursue the theoretical interests of his choosing in a department that was both intellectually and socially supportive of his efforts. Some indication of the important refinement and extension of his position that Kelly was undertaking at Brandeis is preserved in his paper "Ontological Acceleration" (1969), written in the last year of his life. The prospects for major cluster-level development (Mullins, 1973) at Brandeis were made still brighter by the earlier recruitment of Brendan Maher, one of Kelly's former and most respected students. In addition, Kelly brought with him Jack Adams-

Webber, one of the last of his students at Ohio State, thereby transplanting a mature and productive apprenticeship relation into the nascent network. However, Kelly's fatal and untimely heart attack shortly after his arrival at Brandeis deprived the promising network of its social and intellectual leader. The subsequent disintegration of the Brandeis group, perhaps as much as any other social factor, may have retarded the disciplinary development of PCT, especially in this country.

State University of New York–Albany, 1961–present. The pivotal figure in the Albany PCT group has been James Mancuso, a 1958 Rochester Ph.D. who joined the Albany faculty in 1961. Unlike many of the other contributors to the theory, Mancuso never studied directly with Kelly or any of his students. In fact, he did not encounter PCT until late in 1958, when he was practicing in the counseling service at Lehigh University. His earlier work with children in a school setting had convinced Mancuso that the "mechanistic" and "pseudopsychoanalytic" models in which he had been trained had severe limitations. In his search for an alternative, he turned to the works of Piaget and then Kelly, finding in both theories positions that were compatible with the "grass-roots constructivism" of the southern Italian culture in which he was raised. PCT seemed to recognize formally the relativity of social perspectives that was implicit in his childhood play. This same emphasis on constructivism is evident in Mancuso's professional writings concerning children (Mancuso, 1977), in which he encourages the adoption of a "contextualist" model that adequately recognizes the complex social/cognitive factors in human development.

Albany graduated its first contributor to the theory (N. A. Vacc) in 1967 and was strengthened as a center by the addition of W. L. Simmons to the faculty in 1970. Since that time, Albany has graduated two Ph.D.s who have produced important PCT research: Kenneth Handin, who has collaborated with Mancuso on a personal construct approach to parent training (e.g., Mancuso & Handin, 1980), and Uriel Meshoulam, who has followed up F. Fransella's (1972) classic study of stuttering (Meshoulam, 1978). The fact that several additional students (e.g., Bruce Eimer, Karen Hunter, and Richard Leher) have become involved in Macuso's research program suggests that Albany is becoming a major training site in PCT, as well as a research center for interested faculty.

University of Florida, 1967–present. The arrival at Florida of both Franz Epting and David Suchman from Ohio State marked it as a particularly propitious spot for high-level activity in PCT. Epting in particular was quick to establish an ongoing research program in the theory, at first following up on his graduate school interest in cognitive complexity (e.g., Epting & Wilkins, 1974), and later, in conjunction with students, diversifying into such areas as death and dying (e.g., Rigdon, Epting, R. A. Neimeyer & Krieger; Epting & R. Neimeyer, 1984) and parent-child interaction (e.g., Epting, Zempel & Rubio, 1979). The Florida network has shown a consistent ability to attract students at both the graduate (S. Krieger, L. Rainey, M. Rigdon, and G. Wilkins) and undergraduate level (L. Leitner, R. Neimeyer, G. Neimeyer) who published in the theory while still in training. Moreover, Florida's graduate exchange program with the University of Utrecht in the Netherlands gives it an institutional connection with the leading continental European network in PCT (see coauthorship section below). The Dutch network, headed by Han Bonarius, has sent a number of students to study at the American setting, one of whom (P. Dingemans) has already attained contributor status. The recent merger of the personality and counseling programs at Florida may produce a fruitful cross-fertilization of theory and practice in PCT, and should strengthen the collaboration between Epting and Suchman, who previously were in separate areas. The outlook for continued development of the Florida cluster is good, given the 1981 faculty recruitment of Greg Neimeyer, who brought to the group expertise in social as well as counseling psychology.[6]

University of Kansas, 1968–present. The network at Kansas began with the recruitment of Walter Crockett from Clark University in 1968. Crockett had earned his Ph.D. in social psychology in 1953, working under T. Newcomb at Michigan. Like Mancuso, he discovered PCT independently through his reading of Kelly's 1955 work shortly after its publication and found that it articulated well with his pre-existing interest in the "semiphenomenological" thought of Lewin, Snygg, and Coombs. Construct theory, for Crockett, offered a statement of how the individual represented his or her personal "life-space" in terms amenable to experimental investigation.

Crockett's active sponsorship of personal construct research among his students soon made Kansas one of the most vital research centers for the theory in the U.S. The new network was strengthened by the addition of Alan Press, an earlier Clark Ph.D., to Kansas's School of Social Welfare in 1975. Through their interdepartmental collaboration, Crockett and Press were successful in developing a research program that involved numerous students and examined a variety of topics in social cognition and interpersonal communication (e.g., Crockett, Gonyea, & Delia, 1970; Delia, Crockett, Press, & O'Keefe, 1975; Crockett, 1982). The most influential of the students to emerge from this training center was Jesse Delia, who went to establish his own active research center for PCT in the Department of Speech Communications at the University of Illinois–Urbana in 1973.

University of Nebraska–Lincoln, 1972–present. Landfield's move to Nebraska opened up the prospect of developing a major social center in PCT there. His sponsorship of the Clearing House for PCT research, his own high rate of publication, and his sponsorship of the First International Congress in PCT at Nebraska in 1975 all favored such a development. Despite the network's newness, Nebraska has graduated two students, Larry Leitner and myself (both of whom had studied with Epting as undergraduates at Florida), who have gone on to publish in PCT. Several additional students (e.g., A. Colon, C. Schmittdiel) recently have joined the center. A major thrust of the Nebraska group has been the application of personal construct methodologies to the study of such topics as dyadic interaction (Landfield, 1979), nonverbal construing (R. A. Neimeyer, 1981), and the interrelationship of value-related, emotional, and behavioral implications of one's personal constructs (Leitner, 1981). In addition, the Nebraska group has helped to refocus attention on the process of psychotherapy conducted from a PCT perspective (Landfield & Leitner, 1980).

University of Rochester, 1972–present. The pivotal figure in the Rochester PCT network was Rue Cromwell, who assumed a professorship in psychiatry, pediatrics, and psychology at the UR medical school in 1972. Cromwell first became acquainted with construct theory in the early 1950s as a graduate student at OSU, where he did a thesis under Kelly's supervision concerning conceptual clustering in recalling the names of acquaintances. His interest in grid technique continued, and in subsequent positions at Peabody, Vanderbilt, and the LaFayette Clinic (Detroit), Cromwell collaborated with students on further personal construct research (e.g., Cromwell & Caldwell, 1962). It was at LaFayette that Cromwell met L. Space, with whom he worked on a dissertation studying depression from a PCT perspective. Later, upon becoming the chief of the Division of Psychiatry at the University of Rochester School of Medicine, Cromwell was able to hire Space to continue their earlier line of research (Space & Cromwell, 1980) and to initiate others e.g., in schizophrenic cognition (Space & Cromwell, 1978). A distinctive feature of their research program has been the development of a sophisticated, computer-based, interactive program for eliciting and analyzing reptests (Space & Huntzinger, 1979). Along with related work in Great Britain (see chap. 4 below), these technological advancements are likely to revolutionize grid technique in the next decade, enormously expanding the existing range of analyses and applications of grid results.

The research productivity of the Rochester network was augmented in 1978, when Peter Dingemans, from the University of Utrecht (the Netherlands), arrived to do a postdoctoral fellowship. Additional studies of construing processes of schizophrenics followed (Dingemans, Space, & Cromwell, 1983). At the same time, advances were being made on the social front. With the encouragement of Space and Dingemans, Cromwell formed a link with Adams-Webber's PCT network at Brock University in Canada, and subsequently has served as an external Ph.D. advisor to students in the Canadian setting. I also joined the Rochester network in 1981, conducting research in psychotherapy for depression (R. A. Neimeyer, Heath, & Strauss, 1985) before taking a faculty position at Memphis State University in 1983.

Notre Dame, 1977–present. Notre Dame is unique as a research and training center in PCT, in that it is the only such network initiated by a student. As an incoming graduate student in counseling psychology, Greg Neimeyer imported construct theory from the University of Florida where he had studied under Franz Epting. While still at Florida, Greg and I had begun to research the relationship between self-disclosure and psychological construing (R. A. Neimeyer & G. J. Neimeyer, 1977). This work kindled the interest of two Notre Dame faculty members, P. Banikiotes and T. Merluzzi, who had been involved in related social perceptual studies from different theoretical perspectives. In collaboration with various students, G. Neimeyer, Banikiotes, and Merluzzi developed a research program focusing upon self-disclosure and the acquaintance process from a PCT vantage point (Neimeyer, Banikiotes, & Ianni, 1979; Neimeyer & Merluzzi, 1979).

Most of the remaining American contributors to PCT are scattered throughout a variety of academic institutions, usually one in a department. Many (like S. Rosenberg at Rutgers) remain important for their continued research in the theory. Others (like J. Carr at the Uni-

versity of Washington Medical School) serve an important role by intro-
ducing to PCT students who might later seek advanced training or faculty positions at one of the major centers. This pattern of institutionalization of PCT in the U.S. carries implications for the theory group's
degree of maturity as a discipline, a theme that will be elaborated on in
chapter 7 below.

B. Publication Patterns in the United States

The development of a theory group proceeds along multiple lines
simultaneously. On the one hand, there is the social structural progress
made by the group, as reflected, for example, in the establishment of
training and research centers, the subject of the last section. On the
other hand, there is the accumulation of theoretical, empirical, and
applied research in the new style that is published in learned books and
journals. Such research reports are important from a sociological stand-
point because: (1) the number of such reports over time provides one
important gauge of the group's rate of development (Lemaine et al.,
1976, p. 14); and (2) such published work represents one of two "for-
ums" in which the status of the theory group is established. H. M.
Collins and T. J. Pinch (1978) refer to such formal, public work as the
"constitutive" forum—the"objective" contributions of the group to scientific knowledge, the published criticisms of such work, and so on.
Less acknowledged but equally important is the "contingent" forum, in
which "discussion and gossip, fund-raising and publicity seeking, the
setting up and joining of professional organizations, the corralling of
student followers," and similar covert processes contribute to the group's
development or demise. The contingent forum corresponds roughly to
social-structural processes discussed elsewhere in this study. This section will examine publication patterns in PCT in the United States as a
second indicator of the theory group's evolution over time.

The development of a comprehensive bibliography of publications in PCT is detailed in an unpublished manuscript. I sought to
include in the bibliography references to all published books, book
chapters, and articles generated by the theory group over the nearly
thirty years of its existence. Of the 800-plus items in the bibliography,
363 are American. Interpreting the distribution of these by publication
type over time will be the main concern of this chapter.

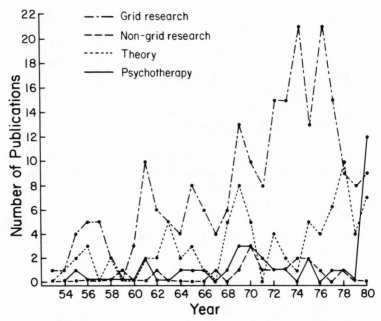

Figure 1. Number of American publications in construct theory by category and year, 1953–1980.

Figure 1 depicts the annual number of American publications in PCT from 1953 to 1980, inclusive. I have broken these down into four nonoverlapping and exhaustive categories for the sake of analysis:

1. *Grid research*. Publications utilizing a variant of Kelly's (1955) Role Construct Repertory Test, Repertory Grid, or derivative procedures (e.g., Bieri's test of "cognitive complexity"). Although this category covers an enormous range of methodologies (Fransella & Bannister, 1977; G. J. Neimeyer & R. A. Neimeyer, 1981a), forms of the grid display more similarities than dissimilarities (e.g., virtually all concentrate on the assessment of an individual's conceptual structure by way of her or his verbal or written report of "bipolar constructs"; most require the sorting of elements in terms of binary or continuous scales flanked by the constructs). Since various forms of the grid are often regarded as the unique psychometric con-

tribution of PCT, I felt that a unitary classification of these procedures was warranted.

2. *Nongrid research.* Empirical work conducted within a PCT framework that relies upon any other research method (e.g., interview, questionnaire, sociogram, behavioral observation) rather than the grid.

3. *Theory.* Writing that delineates or expands upon the basic conceptual framework of PCT or applies this framework to the theoretical analysis of a given content area.

4. *Psychotherapy.* Discussions of the clinical procedures following from PCT, or applications of them to a particular case. Case studies reporting grid results for the client or patient were categorized under "grid research" above.

Obviously, several alternative classificatory schemes could have been used to categorize such references. For example, papers could have been classed on the basis of the content areas they addressed, the rigor of the research design or logic employed, the age of the individuals with whom they dealt, and so on. Each such scheme would have its intrinsic strengths and weaknesses. I chose to focus on the formal properties of the reports (i.e., the *category* of work) because such a classification promised to shed light on the *style* of research preferred by construct theorists and the relative contributions to theory, empirical work, and applied psychology made by the group, while at the same time retaining the advantages of clarity and simplicity.

Several features of the data displayed in figure 1 are of interest. Perhaps the most striking is the overall increase, despite the year-to-year variations, in the quantity of grid research conducted from the 1950s to the 1970s. (The "drop-off" in articles in recent years is more apparent than real, owing to the lag time in incorporating publications into the bibliography.) This exponential increase in the average number of grid publications annually (from 3.2 in the mid-1950s to 17 in the mid-1970s) accords with Price's (1961) estimates of the output of successful scientific disciplines and suggests that PCT has continued to gain momentum on the empirical front in this country. Interest in grid research seems to peak in four- or five-year cycles, although it is not immediately clear why this should be the case. Some such upsurges in interest seem to follow the publication of major position statements; Kelly's original exposition of the theory in 1955, Bannister and Mair's

Evaluation of Personal Constructs in 1968, Landfield's *Personal Construct Systems in Psychotherapy* in 1971. It may be that the periodic appearance of such intellectual successes on the American scene (the Bannister and Mair book, though British in authorship, became the leading methodological handbook in the U.S. as well) spurred a general interest in grid work within the research community.

In sharp contrast to the vitality of PCT research relying upon grid techniques is the infrequent and uneven production of PCT research utilizing *any other* methodology. This reliance upon a single set of methodologies for conducting empirical work leaves the theory in a vulnerable position, the advantages of the repertory grid notwithstanding (see chap. 8 below). Despite the still smaller number of nongrid studies being performed, the bulk of these has been done since 1970, suggesting a growing effort within the American PCT community toward greater methodological diversification.

The volume of *theoretical* work produced by the group also shows a discernable increase since the mid-1950s (averaging over six publications annually in the last five years as opposed to only one annually in the first five years charted). Theoretical writing seemed to crest in the mid and the late 1960s, and seems to be experiencing a renaissance since the late 1970s. At no point, however, has it outstripped the production of grid research. This is worth noting, because some construct theorists assume that an overemphasis on theory was largely responsible for the slow uptake on Kelly's ideas on the part of American psychologists. Adams-Webber, for example, contends:

> At an early stage in the development of this PCT model . . . there emerged a tendency to rush on into the discussion phase before completing the experimentation and systematic assessment needed to write a 'results section.' It was perhaps the lack of results which, for a long period of time, retarded the development of interest in personal construct theory, especially in North America, where results are always of paramount importance. (1979, p. xi)

If a purely quantitative comparison of empirical and theoretical work has any bearing on this claim, then an explanation of America's early reluctance to embrace PCT must be sought in other factors.

Finally, Figure 1 depicts the sporadic attention given by American construct theorists to the topic of psychotherapy. Despite the undeniable historical roots of the theory in clinical psychology, there has been a surprising dearth of detailed case studies of the sort that comprises a large percentage of the literature in other clinically based theory groups, e.g., psychoanalysis and applied behavior analysis. When case reports appear, they typically concentrate on reporting grid findings concerning the client, often before and after therapy. Such reports are valuable, but they fail to give sufficient attention to largely unexplored potential contributions of PCT to psychotherapeutic practice. Fortunately, American interest in PCT's clinical relevance is on a dramatic upswing, as recent volumes by Landfield and Leitner (1980) and Epting (1984) demonstrate.

Figure 2 gives a breakdown of American PCT publications by source, from 1953 to the present. As was true of figure 1, this graph reflects the continued growth of the theory group's literature, particularly over the last decade. It also suggests the important role that books

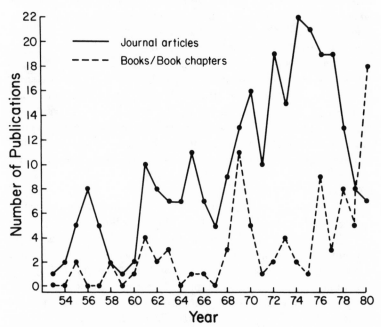

Figure 2. Number of American publications in construct theory by source and year, 1953–1980.

and book chapters have played in the publication patterns of the group since its inception. Many of these were chapters contributed by Kelly or his students to books edited by other psychologists. However, six volumes devoted exclusively to PCT had been authored or edited by American construct theorists through 1980. The first of these, of course, was Kelly's cornerstone work, published by Norton in 1955, which has been available continuously since that time. In 1963, Norton reissued the first three (introductory) chapters to this work as a separate paperback, thereby making available for the first time a text in PCT suitable for widespread course adoption. In 1969, Maher secured the posthumous publication of several of Kelly's addresses and papers, and in so doing established Wiley as a reliable outlet for the work of the theory group both in the U.S. and abroad. Over the last ten years, Landfield has emerged as a major social and intellectual leader in the theory, arranging for the publication of three volumes since 1971. These include his extensive outcome research in psychotherapy (Landfield, 1971), the proceedings of the Nebraska Symposium on Motivation on PCT (Landfield, 1977), and a co-edited collection of original papers on PCT in psychotherapy (Landfield & Leitner, 1980).

Figure 2 also indicates that PCT articles published in American journals have proliferated more rapidly than have book and chapter publications (the apparent sharp decline in number of articles in the late 1970s being artifactual because of delays in incorporating recent work into the bibliography). This is important in terms of the field's development, since journals have the advantage (generally) of reaching a wider and more diverse readership, whereas specialized books primarily serve as durable intellectual resources for scientists already working within the theory group.

Something of the status of PCT vis-a-vis American academic psychology can be gleaned from table 2, which lists the five U.S. journals in which construct theorists most frequently publish. Of these, three (*Journal of Abnormal and Social Psychology, Journal of Clinical and Consulting Psychology,* and *Journal of Counseling Psychology*) are "mainline" American Psychological Association publications. The other two are journals commanding less respect in the academic community. The fact that these less prestigious journals are the first and third most common outlets for PCT articles in the U.S., coupled with the finding that 72 percent of PCT articles in this country appear in non-APA publications, suggests that American construct theorists have

---

Table 2
American journals in which personal construct theory articles
are published most frequently, 1953–1980.

Journal	# of articles	% of U.S. PCT articles
Psychological Reports	28	10.1
Journal of Abnormal (and Social) Psychology	23	8.3
Perceptual and Motor Skills	22	8.0
Journal of Consulting and Clinical Psychology	16	5.8
Journal of Counseling Psychology	16	5.8

Note: 28% of American journal articles in PCT appear in American Psychological Association publications.

---

had difficulty penetrating the major journals in their own country. Why
this may be so will be taken up in a later chapter.

By way of summary, table 3 displays the total number of American PCT publications, partitioned by both category and source. It is
evident from the table that the group's greatest contributions (at least
quantitatively) have been in the areas of grid research and theory. Papers
devoted to psychotherapy have been rare (only thirty-three papers in
twenty-seven years). Of more serious concern is the stylistically re-
stricted empirical base on which the theory has been erected, at least in
this country. Although nearly two hundred fifty research publications in
PCT have appeared in the U.S., an incredible 93 percent of these have
relied upon some form of the repertory grid as the primary (or more
often the *only*) means of operationalizing the variables being studied.
The implications of this disproportionate reliance on a single measurement technique will be explored further below.

Table 3
Number of American publications in personal construct theory by category and source, 1953–1980.

	Books/ Chapters	Journal Articles	Total	%
Grid research	25	205	230	63
Nongrid research	0	16	16	5
Theory	43	41	84	23
Psychotherapy	19	14	33	9
Total	87	276	363	
Percentage	24	76		

Note: Total number of empirical publications (grid and nongrid) is 246, or 68% of all published work. Of these, 230 (93%) utilize some form of grid.

C. Coauthorship Networks in the United States

Of the four forms of social-communicative ties outlined by Mullins (1973), those based upon coauthorship are perhaps the closest, requiring that the people involved coordinate ideas, research, and writing. Those based on informal communication may be of short or long duration and varying importance, perhaps markedly influencing the thought of one or both parties. However, unless they eventuate in mutually sponsored research or theorizing, the impact of such associations on the theory group as a whole may be limited. Similarly, colleagueship in itself need not imply a particularly close or fruitful collaborative relationship; and apprenticeship, except at its most advanced stages, lacks the mutuality that characterizes most coauthorship. For this reason, examining coauthorship networks can yield important information concerning the degree of social structural cohesiveness displayed by a theory group as it evolves. This section will present and comment upon such networks as they have developed among construct theorists in the United States.

Figure 3 represents the coauthorship pattern among American construct theorists from 1954 to 1980. The dates of particular coauthor ties are indicated by the type of line connecting the two (or more) figures in question. For example, the figure indicates that Landfield and Epting

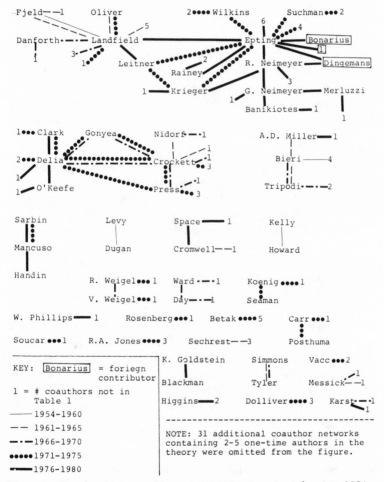

Figure 3. Coauthorship networks among American construct theorists, 1954–1980.

jointly wrote one or more published papers between 1976 and 1980, that Landfield coauthored with Danforth at least once between 1966 and 1970, and so on. For the sake of simplicity, only those persons publishing at least twice in PCT are indicated by name in the figure; persons coauthoring only once with a contributor for a particular five-year period are represented only by their number. Thirty-one networks composed of persons publishing only once in the theory were omitted from the figure.

Overall, the coauthorship map suggests that members of American PCT theory group have remained only loosely connected. Most of the authors exist in small, isolated pockets, seldom containing more than two significant contributors. There are only three important exceptions. The first is the largely extinct network surrounding Bieri, whose research program focused on the variable of cognitive complexity. Bannister and Mair have observed that the study of this variable by the use of grid technique, though originating in PCT, has become "virtually a self-contained research area" (1968, p. 70). The absence of coauthorship links between members of the Bieri group and any other American construct theorists would support this contention.

A second, larger network was organized around Crockett at Kansas, whose work has dealt with impression formation and various other social perceptual topics. Although some of its members have become inactive as personal construct researchers since 1975, the group as a whole has remained prolific under the shared intellectual leadership of Delia, who broadened its base of operations to the University of Illinois.[7]

The third and largest coauthorship network represents the core of active American PCT researchers. The group has at its hub Landfield and Epting, the two most published living construct theorists in the U.S., and includes several high-producing, second-generation authors as well. Actually, the network developed from the growing together of two smaller groups. The first, which was active from the mid-1950s to the early 1970s, was organized by Landfield at the University of Missouri. This group concentrated primarily upon psychotherapy research and methodological concerns. The second, and still-expanding, group includes Epting at the University of Florida and several of his ex-students who have coauthored a number of articles pertaining to the measurement of death threat. The Florida subgroup also contains authors who have collaborated with Epting on more traditional investigations (e.g., cognitive complexity). The group has annexed the emerging Notre Dame center with its research program in interpersonal attraction and self-disclosure. The Landfield and Epting subgroups merged in the last four years when the longtime informal communication link between the two men eventuated in joint publications. This linkage was reinforced by subsequent coauthorship between Landfield (then at Nebraska) and his former student Leitner, who had studied and written with Epting as an undergraduate.

It is worth noting that American coauthorship networks have remained largely unconnected to similar networks in other countries. The only exceptions to this are the coauthor links forged recently between participants in the American theory group on the one hand, and prominent members of the Dutch construct theory group on the other. This development is a promising one if it represents a growing cognizance of the value of international cooperation in conducting research.

A close examination of the annual number of coauthorship links indicates that they doubled in quantity for each of the successive five-year periods from the late 1950s to the early 1970s, and have remained numerous since that time. This pattern of exponential growth in the density of such ties is consistent with Mullins's (1973) model, which hold that coauthorship becomes an increasingly important form of social structural "cement" as the group matures to clusterhood.

4

PERSONAL CONSTRUCT THEORY IN GREAT BRITAIN

A. British Research and Training Centers

Approximately a decade after Kelly began formulating the outlines of his theory in the U.S., his ideas began to draw international
attention. By the late 1950s, PCT had begun to attract adherents in
Great Britain, and by the mid-1960s it was being vigorously debated,
applied, and elaborated by a small but devoted network of psychologists
and psychiatrists there. Despite its more recent origin, the British theory
group has grown rapidly, so that by 1980 as many British as American
authors had attained contributor status (i.e., published at least twice in
the theory). Table 4 presents these contributors.

As is true of construct theory in the United States, PCT in Great
Britain is a predominately clinical specialty: 54 percent of construct
theorists in the latter country hold clinical psychology degrees, compared with 56 percent in the U.S. Roughly 25 percent of British theory
group members were trained as academic psychologists (in developmental, social, and experimental areas), with social psychologists alone constituting nearly 20 percent of the total theory group. In contrast to their
American counterparts, 18 percent of whom come from (chiefly academic) fields outside psychology, British construct theorists rarely seem
to hold terminal degrees in other fields. The only important exception is

Table 4
Contributors to PCT: Great Britain

Agnew, J.	Hay, J. A.	Radley, A. R.
Applebee, A. N.	Heather, N. (B.)	Ravenette, A. T.
Bannister, D.	Holland, R.	Reid, F.
Barden, V.	Honess, T. M.	Rohde, P. D.
Bender, M. P.	Hope, K.	Rowe, D.
Breen, D.	Hay, R. M.	Ryle, A.
Buckley, F.	Jones, H. G.	Salmon, Ph.
Craig, G.	Kushner, A. W.	Sarre, P.
Caine, T. M.	Lauterbach, W.	Shapiro, D. A.
Canter, D. V.	Lemon, N.	Shaw, M. L.
Caplan, H. L.	Lipshitz, S.	Slater, P.
Chetwynd, S. J.	Lunghi, M. E.	Smail, D. J.
Crisp, A. H.	Mair, J. M. M.	Spelman, M. S.
Downs, R. M.	Maklouf-Norris, F.	Stringer, P.
Draffan, J. W.	McFayden, M.	Thomas, L. F.
Duck, S. W.	McPherson, F. M.	Warr, P. B.
Foulds, G. A.	Mellsop, G. W.	Warren, N.
Fransella, F.	Moss, A. E.	Watson, J. P.
Frost, W. A. K.	Norris, H.	Williams, E.
Harri-Augstein, S.	Phillip, A. E.	Winter, D. A.
Harrison, A. W.	Phillips, J. P.	Wood, R. R.
Harrison, J.	Poole, A. D.	Wooster, A. D.
	Presley, A. S.	

the 10 percent of British contributors who are psychiatrists, a field completely unrepresented by theory group members in the U.S., at least until 1980. As will be evident below, this international difference in composition of the two subgroups may carry implications for other aspects of their sociohistorical development, e.g., the publication outlets utilized by group members and the institutional footholds each attained within the university systems of their respective countries.

University of London, 1957–present. In examining the institutionalization of PCT in the U.K., it is important to recognize that the structure of the British university system is fundamentally different from the American model, in a sense is almost the reverse. In the U.S., the university exists as a cohesive sociopolitical entity, whose separate colleges (e.g., arts and letters, business, science, and technology) exist primarily on paper, often sharing students and, to some extent, even physical facilities. As such, the colleges and the departments which comprise them are largely subordinated to a central administration. In contrast, the major universities in Great Britain (e.g., Oxford, Cambridge, University of London) exist only in a much looser bureaucratic sense as degree-granting institutions. The colleges of which they consist are virtually autonomous; each has its own historical roots, its own departments, its own faculty and student body. Thus, the University of London is actually a system of several free-standing colleges (e.g., Chelsea, Bedford and Kings Colleges, the London School of Economics) and university-affiliated hospitals (e.g., Maudesley, Middlesex, Guys, Royal Free) where medical and related clinical specialties (including clinical psychology) are housed. Despite the fact that construct theorists with University of London affiliations often work in separate institutions, I have chosen to discuss them here as members of a single research and training center. This seems appropriate, given that the geographical proximity of the various colleges allows construct theorists within the London area to achieve a much closer coordination of activities (e.g., seminars, research, supervision) than theory group members working in geographically-remote institutions in the U.S. The synergism resulting from such collaboration helps account for the rapid growth of British construct theory over the last two decades.

The introduction of personal construct theory into Great Britain stems to a remarkable extent from the work of one man, Don Bannister. Bannister chanced upon Kelly's initial two volumes in 1957, while he was studying for his doctorate at the University of London's Maudesley Hospital. Because of its eventual significance for the history of PCT, Bannister's first encounter with the theory is worth examining in greater detail. While studying for his predoctoral examinations, he was literally reading through the library collection of personality texts in alphabetical order when he came across Kelly's recently published magnum opus:

> I was looking for a framework . . . that would enable me to fight and survive in the middle of what to me was a very unsympathetic [behaviorist] setting. And sometime during the '50's' I got to "Kelly." Thank god his name wasn't Zininsky! But I finally got to the K's, and Kelly. I remember getting the two volumes, finding them at the library, and taking them back to my office. . . . It was a Sunday morning. And I read straight through the day, until about 8 or 9 in the evening. And I

quite *liked* what I was reading, but I didn't quite see . . . I mean, it was fine, but. . . . And I liked the kind of joking approach to things, and I liked some of the sort of insights, and so on. I remember thinking it was a pretty *grand* theory. But umm, I was quite able to gladly put the book down at 8 and go home. But something happened when I got home. I walked right into the house, and there was nobody in the living room, and the television was on. And I was too tired to switch it off, and just sort of slumped down on the sofa and stared at it. And it was the religious channel, it being Sunday. . . . and I sat there gazing at it. Without quite realizing what I was doing, I found myself saying things like, "That's a pretty loose construct! I'm not sure how he's going to validate a construction of that kind." And I went on and on like that. And then suddenly I realized what I was doing, that I was making sense of what he was saying in those terms. And this really did sort of seize hold of me, because one of the part-articulated demands I'd been taught or read about was a sort of personal demand, that they somehow make sense of me and my personal life. Yeah, this was a pretty intransigent demand. And most of them, well, they didn't meet it at all. I mean, a lot of them either seemed just not to mention me, they didn't mention anything that *I* could cling onto, or else were downright insulting about me. That was so for psychoanalytic theory and learning theory both. I just will not have it, I'm sorry. So that really kind of stuck in my mind. So then I went back on Monday, and I read faster and harder. . . . And that would have been my first day's encounter. That would have been about the middle of 1957, I suppose. (Bannister, 1979, personal communication)

Bannister's remarks here are significant because they illustrate that his acceptance of the theory was based on its relevance to *his life*, and the everyday events that constituted it. Moreover, it clearly took the form of a *personal commitment* to a form of knowledge (c.f. Polanyi, 1964), one that was all the more clearly impassioned because of his being situated in a social/professional milieu inimical to his position. While not universal, these same factors were operative in the attraction the theory held for the great majority of the most visible construct theorists, especially those of the "first generation" (i.e., those who studied directly under Kelly or were the peers, in age, of those who did). Unfortunately, space limitations preclude supporting and elaborating this theme with material from other interviews. Suffice it to say that PCT's "reflexivity" has been a primary source of its appeal among its adherents. Thus, from the late 1950s on, Bannister found himself taken with the theory's reflexivity, and its capacity to apply meaningfully to his own life, and with its active and respectful image of persons. While at the Maudesley, Bannister began his pioneering work in schizophrenic thought disorder from a PCT perspective (Bannister, 1960). In 1958 he sent the results of his pilot studies to Kelly at OSU. A long silence followed, which finally was ended by the arrival of a reply from Kelly, who had circulated the studies to his graduate seminars for a detailed critique and brainstorming regarding directions in which the research might be taken. A sporadic correspondence continued between the two men until 1960, when Kelly visited England and lectured at the Maudesley at Bannister's invitation.

Bannister began functioning as a social leader in British PCT even during his graduate years at U London. His enthusiasm for the new theory proved to be contagious, as younger graduate students read and discussed the tenets of Kelly's position with him. Tom Ravenette, for example, borrowed the first of Kelly's (1955) volumes from Bannister and immediately found in it "a rounded set of ideas which [he] could carry forward into the practice of educational psychology" (Ravenette, 1979, personal communication). In his subsequent work he has continued to develop the implications of personal construct theory and methodology for the assessment and treatment of children's problems, especially in the school setting (e.g., Ravenette, 1968, 1975, 1977, 1980).

Bannister's zeal for PCT had a similarly long-lasting impact upon Miller Mair, who arrived at the Maudesley in 1959 from the University of Aberdeen, just as Bannister was completing his dissertation. In the course of his social relationship with Bannister, Mair discovered Kelly's writing and began reading it with "incredible excitement" (Mair, 1979, personal communication). For the next several years as a student and then a faculty member at U London, Mair conducted detailed critical studies of repertory grid technique (e.g., Mair, 1966, 1967), a line of research that culminated in his coauthorship with Bannister of the theory's first major methodological handbook (Bannister & Mair, 1968). Like many construct theorists who begin their careers by doing an "apprenticeship" in grid technique, Mair recently has turned his attention to increasingly theoretical and philosophical issues (e.g., Mair, 1970a, 1970b, 1979).

Although Bannister left the Maudesley in 1960 to take a position at Bexley, a National Health Service hospital not officially affiliated with the U London system, his influence upon incoming students continued. A case in point is his relationship with Fay Fransella, who was studying clinical psychology at the Maudesley in 1962 when Bannister returned for a visit. In part as a result of such social contact, she later decided to adopt grid technique as a means of operationalizing the self-understanding of stutterers (Fransella, 1972). She began to read seriously Kelly's *theory* when she discovered that her grid results were uninterpretable divorced from their conceptual context (Fransella, 1979, personal communication). Like Mair, Fransella has gone on to do a considerable amount of writing in PCT (e.g., Fransella, 1969, 1970, 1974, 1976, 1978, 1980), and has collaborated with Bannister on an important manual for grid technique (Fransella & Bannister, 1977) as well as an introductory text (Bannister & Fransella, 1971). Along with Mair, she also has come to share with Bannister the leadership of the growing British theory group.

By the mid-1960s PCT was well enough represented among U London faculty and students to offer a competing paradigm to the "passionate behaviorism" that then prevailed at the university. The presence of Patrick Slater on the faculty (at U London's Institute of Psychiatry) was especially important. Slater had taken his doctorate at the university in 1960 at the age of 51 and went on to accept a faculty appointment at the institution. Shortly thereafter, he was introduced to PCT by F. Maklouf, an Egyptian student who had heard about repertory grids from Bannister and wanted to employ them in a research design. This provided the impetus for Slater, who was well versed in statistics and computer technology, to adapt the methods employed by his (1960) dissertation research to the analysis of grids (Slater, 1965). His computerized principal components programs quickly became popular among researchers, since they provided an expedient and clinically rich alternative to the manual scoring methods then available (Kelly, 1955; Bannister, 1960). Slater's programs played a crucial role in maintaining British interest in PCT, particularly after the Medical Research Council made them accessible to psychiatrists and psychologists throughout the U.K. As Dorothy Rowe, a member of the London group, explained, "Don Bannister's work was interesting—people loved to listen to Don talk— but the computer gave them something to hold onto" (Rowe, 1979, personal communication). Unfortunately, the complementary theoretical and technical prowess of Bannister and Slater failed to lead to a collaborative relationship. In part, this was the result of Bannister's preference for simpler, hand-calculated analyses that remained more closely tied to raw grid data, and in part it followed from Slater's being "less interested in the area covered by the theory outside the limits of the technique" (Slater, 1979, personal communication). In spite of this rift between the two figures, a number of U London researchers have managed to integrate construct *theory* with Slater's (1977) techniques to investigate a wide variety of clinical and social psychological topics in recent years (e.g., Chetwynd, 1976; Norris & Maklouf-Norris, 1976; Phillips, Cashdan, Flynn, & Meadows, 1979; Rowe, 1976; Stringer, 1976).

By the early 1970s, the U London cluster had grown to include several faculty and numerous students who were active in PCT research. Some students continued research along traditional lines, e.g., in schizophenic thought disorder (Poole, 1976, 1979). Others broke new ground in areas such as classroom assessment (Wood & Napthali, 1975), market research (Frost & Braine, 1967), developmental psychology (Applebee, 1975, 1976; Salmon, 1969, 1976, 1979; Wooster, 1970), and group therapy (Caplan, Rhode, Shapiro, & Watson, 1975; Smail, 1972; Watson, 1970, 1972). At least one student, Alan Radley, has done significant work in both traditional and nontraditional areas. Radley had become imbued with construct theory during his undergraduate years (1964–1968) at Brunel, where he studied with Laurie Thomas and others acquainted with PCT. Having done an undergraduate project on serial invalidation and thought disorder in schizophrenia, he was offered a research position by Bannister upon graduation. He accepted the offer and in 1972 entered the U London research group while simultaneously working toward a doctorate in clinical psychology at the Middlesex Hospital Medical School. This position involved Radley closely with both Bannister, who served as his director of studies, and Mair, who was his supervisor. Their research program eventuated in a series of studies on schizophrenic thought disorder (Bannister, Adams-Webber, Penn, & Radley, 1975; Radley, 1974a, 1974b). After earning his degree, however, Radley (like Mair) began writing on more theoretical and metatheoretical themes, sometimes challenging and refining PCT's fundamental assumptions (Radley, 1977, 1978a, 1978b, 1979).

A roughly parallel course of development was followed by Peter Stringer, a faculty member at U London's University College from 1966 to 1972. Stringer first learned of PCT when he met Bannister in 1962 at the house of a mutual friend. Over the next two years, he read occasional articles in the theory and attended Bannister's PCT symposium at the British Psychological Society's Annual Conference. But he did not become deeply involved in the new approach until 1964, when Neil Warren sponsored a series of PCT seminars at Brunel University (see below). Stringer, like Mair and Radley, was attracted first to the methodology associated with the repertory grid and applied it to problems of architectual and environmental perception (Stringer, 1970, 1971). In recent years, however, he has become increasingly interested in metatheoretical issues, such as the relationship of persons to the social roles they occupy (Stringer, 1979).

Just as the work of the London-based group has tended to grow more theoretical and diverse over the years, it also has grown more self-critical. Radley's developing critique of Kelly's treatment of such concepts as "anticipation" and "preverbal construing" already has been noted. In a similar vein, Ray Holland has undertaken an extensive analysis of Kelly's out-of-hand dismissal of competing theorists, ranging from the behaviorists and sociologists to the psychoanalysts and phenomenologists (Holland, 1970, 1977). His criticism of the intellectual tactics of Kelly and others in the PCT camp takes place against a background of general support and enthusiasm for the theory, which he first encountered in the late 1960s by way of his wife's studying with Bannister. The net effect of Holland's critique of PCT may be to render it a more adequate and comprehensive theory by opening it to the inclusion of the insights of thinkers in other disciplines, particularly concerning social issues.

While some members of the U London research cluster have preferred to do the majority of their writing alone, others have contributed to the cohesiveness of the group through extensive coauthorship. A good example is A. H. Crisp, whose early individual work was concerned with a grid-based operationalization of therapeutic "transference," an analytic concept incorporated by Kelly (Crisp, 1964a, 1964b). Since then he has collaborated with Mair in expounding the usefulness of grid technique in clinical practice (Mair & Crisp, 1968) and with Fransella in conducting a series of studies on anorexia and obesity (Crisp & Fransella, 1972; Fransella & Crisp, 1970, 1979).

In summary, the University of London group has produced voluminous research in a variety of substantive and theoretical areas. It also has functioned as the primary training center for construct theorists in Great Britain, including among its students or faculty the majority of those persons who have become significant contributors to the theory in the U.K. Like Ohio State, the first and largest training and research center in the U.S., the U London cluster owes its creation and development to a considerable degree to the work of one man. This is reflected in the fact that most of the major figures at the center (e.g., Ravenette, Mair, Fransella, Salmon, Stringer) first became acquainted with Kelly's work through social or professional contact with Bannister and often continued to collaborate with him on major products. Unlike Ohio State, however, U London has proven durable enough to survive the loss of its founder, who moved from the Maudesley to Bexley Hospital in 1960 (still in the London area but not part of the university system), and who in 1974 moved to High Royds Hospital in Ilkley, three hundred kilometers to the north. Of course, it must be conceded that Bannister has had continued, though less frequent, contact with many of its members. While this may help account for the stability of the group, a more important factor may be the group's success in recruiting other faculty (e.g., Mair, Fransella, Salmon, Crisp, Slater) into the theory group, something that was never accomplished at Ohio State. U London's ability to attract faculty-level researchers can be traced in turn to (1) the appeal of a respectable and highly visible research paradigm based on repertory grid technique, and (2) the structure of the British university, which permitted promising students to be hired by other colleges or hospitals within the U London system following the completion of their doctorates. Neither condition applied to the OSU center. Grid research was less well established in the U.S., in part because popular computerized analysis programs comparable to Slater's had not been developed. In addition, despite its leadership in the training of clinical psychologists in the postwar period, OSU was small by comparison with the U London system, so that virtually all of its graduates were forced by the exigencies of the job market to seek employment elsewhere. A final factor that may explain the differential stability of the American and British centers concerns the respective roles of their founders. Bannister, for all his massive influence in the theory's development, is not the *originator* of PCT. This fact may have permitted others (especially Fransella, Mair, and Salmon) to work more or less *beside* him as colleagues and eventually come to share with him some of the responsibilities of social and intellectual leadership for the growing group. In contrast, Kelly in a sense had no peers; because he was the sole author of the theory, even established investigators necessarily became his *stu-*

dents to the extent that they involved themselves in learning and elaborating his position. Kelly's practice of addressing his students as "Mr." or "Miss" so-and-so and requiring that they address him as "Dr. Kelly" seemed to reinforce this distinction, so that long after their graduation, even many of his most distinguished students found it quite impossible to address Kelly by his first name. Because Kelly clearly remained *the* leader of the American theory group, other Americans at OSU and elsewhere naturally refrained from assuming leadership positions until after his death. Ironically, Kelly's death in 1967, though it undoubtedly slowed the development of PCT in the U.S., may ultimately have strengthened it by encouraging a less hierarchical social structure among group members, one more in line with that existing in Great Britain.

Bexley Hospital, 1960–1972. Following his graduation from the Maudesley in 1959, Bannister took a position at Bexley, a hospital that was part of the National Health Service system in London but that had no close institutional ties with the university. He was successful in soliciting funds to continue his research on the serial invalidation hypothesis of thought disorder and pursued this line of research (Bannister, 1962, 1963, 1965) alone for a few years until he was joined by Phillida Salmon. Salmon had been working at Bexley as a senior clinical psychologist since 1961, when she joined the staff at Bannister's encouragement. For three years she had remained somewhat distant from Bannister's research *per se*, often engaging in friendly debate with him about construct theory's apparent "lack of depth," its seeming inadequacy in dealing with the unconscious, relatively unchanging dynamics of individuals (Salmon, 1979, personal communication). All the while, however, she was "assimilating" the general viewpoint of PCT and finding it to be a refreshing alternative to the medical/diagnostic model in which she had been trained. Finally, when Bannister's grant expired, she approached him with the suggestion that he renew it and request funds to include her as a coinvestigator. For the next four years she worked closely with him, elaborating PCT's application to schizophrenia and other clinical topics (e.g., Bannister & Salmon, 1966; Bannister, Salmon, & Lieberman, 1964).

At about the same time, the research program was strengthened both by the recruitment of A. S. Presley to the Bexley team (see table 4) and by Bannister's collaboration with Fransella at U London. The net result of these joint efforts was a refinement of the group's testing procedures for assessing thought disorder (Bannister & Fransella, 1965; Bannister, Fransella, & Agnew, 1971; Salmon, Bromley, & Presley, 1967).

Bexley's importance as a research and training center began to wane after 1967–1968, when both Salmon and Presley left to take positions elsewhere. Bannister continued the line of research in schizophrenia, however (e.g., Bannister, 1972, 1976), and successfully involved several students in the U London system in this effort, as noted earlier. More significantly, he continued to broaden his contribution to PCT beyond this focal area, both while at Bexley and following his move to High Royds Hospital in 1974. To date, his writing touches on such wide-ranging topics as physiological psychology (Bannister, 1969), psychotherapy (Bannister, 1975), the nature of psychological science (Bannister, 1970a), child development (Bannister & Agnew, 1977), emotionality (Bannister, 1977), and politics (Bannister, 1979). It is probably not an exaggeration to state that Bannister has done more than any other single person, including Kelly, to promote the visibility of PCT in the psychological community. Not only has he been prolific in writing traditional and nontraditional articles and book chapters, but he also has drawn attention to PCT through his spirited verbal and printed debate with Hans Eysenck (Bannister, 1970b). As a result of such activity, he has become the second most frequently cited British psychologist (after Eysenck).

Nevertheless, it would be misleading to assume that Bannister's efforts have been solely responsible for the development of PCT in the U.K. For one thing, subscribing to an oversimplified "great man" theory to explain the group's development risks underemphasizing the importance of a receptive Zeitgeist in the British intellectual community. Although British psychology at midcentury was still strongly identified with the logical-empiricism of Anglo-Saxon metascience (c.f. Radnitsky, 1973), there was a growing discontent with the restrictions such philosophical pronouncements placed upon scientific research (e.g., Polanyi, 1958; Kuhn, 1962), especially in the human sciences. While some British psychologists and psychiatrists of the period (e.g., R. D. Laing, Esterson, and Cooper) made a complete break with empiricism and positivism, aligning themselves instead with continental phenomenological and hermeneutic traditions grounded in the work of Husserl and Sartre, such a break was too radical for most. For many, construct theory's arrival on the psychological scene offered an ideal compromise solution to their dilemma. Its theoretical structure echoed some of the phenomenalism and existentialism of the attractive, but "excessive" European schools (albeit in diluted form, c.f. Holland, 1970). More significantly, PCT's associated grid technique allowed such investigators to operationalize "cognitive" variables in a respectable, imminently quantitative way. Thus, the new theory being propounded by Bannister and others provided the conceptual and technical tools that enabled such researchers to edge comfortably toward a revised paradigm, without requiring of them an abrupt break with their past.[1]

Attributing PCT's development in Britain too exclusively to Bannister's efforts would be misleading for a second reason as well. A number of other British figures have contributed to the theory's social and intellectual development, some of whom have had little contact with Bannister or his circle of coworkers at U London. A discussion of some of the research centers established by these individuals follows.

Brunel University, 1963–present. Neil Warren, a graduate student in social psychology at Brunel in the early 1960s, has been described as "the one person in Britain who knew about construct theory without Don Bannister having told him about it," either directly or indirectly, by way of students (Radley, 1979, personal communication). Upon graduation in 1963, Warren took a faculty position at Brunel for a brief time and arranged a series of "Kelly seminars" that culminated in 1964 in the first significant conference in the new theory outside the U.S. (see chap. 6). Kelly himself presented at the small symposium, an act that helped to catalyze the development of the emerging British theory group and that inaugurated Brunel as a significant research center in PCT.

Despite his early social leadership in the U.K., Warren did not materialize as a major intellectual contributor to the theory, although he did remain involved in its development after his move to the University of Sussex in 1966. Fortunately for the Brunel center, one of Warren's cohorts, Laurie Thomas, emerged as an energetic proponent of Kelly's position. Thomas's Brunel-based Center for the Study of Human Learning, and its offshoot, the Barbican Research Group, have produced a number of recent applications of personal construct methods to various educational and managerial problems, broadly defined (e.g., Beard, 1978; Harri-Augstein, 1978; Pope, 1978; Pope & Keen, 1981; Pope & Shaw, 1981; Thomas, 1978). In addition, like the Rochester research center in the U.S., it has pioneered in the development of sophisticated interactive programs that have established the "state of the art" in computerized grid technique.

Since its inception in the early 1960s, the Brunel center has produced a number of students (e.g., Shaw, Radley) who have gone on to attain significant contributor status. Although it does not rival the U London group in size, it seems likely to play a continued role in the training of future British construct theorists.

University of Sussex, 1964–present. In 1964 Anthony Ryle, an Oxford-trained psychiatrist, assumed the directorship of the University of Sussex Health Service, and promptly initiated a research program on psychotherapy outcome. Although he had begun his pilot work with the Semantic Differential, Ryle converted to the repertory grid after reading Crisp's (1964) paper employing the technique to investigate transference. He proceeded to study the writings of Kelly and Bannister but remained primarily occupied with using techniques derived from PCT to operationalize concepts stemming from psychoanalytic and object-relations approaches (Ryle, 1975). Like Slater, Ryle sees himself as "one of the rather unrespectable repertory grid users who remain somewhat detached from the theory itself" (Ryle, 1980, personal communication). This evaluation notwithstanding, Ryle has done a great deal of theoretically relevant clinical research (e.g., Ryle, 1975, 1976, 1979a, 1979b). More important, he has orchestrated an ongoing research program with three primary collaborators, Martin Lunghi, Dana Breen, and Susan Lipshitz. With Lunghi, he has employed grid techniques to assess therapeutic change (Ryle & Lunghi, 1969), measure therapist empathy (Ryle & Lunghi, 1971) and study student sex-role identification (Ryle & Lunghi, 1972). He and Breen further modified an earlier "dyad" grid (Ryle & Lunghi, 1970) in order to measure the ability of spouses to construe one another's construing (Ryle & Breen, 1972a, 1972b). Finally, he has collaborated with Lipshitz in employing PCT techniques to refine the study of countertransference (Ryle & Lipshitz, 1974), and to study progress in both dyadic (Ryle & Lipshitz, 1975, 1976a) and group therapies (Ryle & Lipshitz, 1976b). In spite of this outpouring of grid research, the group has remained committed to a psychoanalytic theoretical perspective, as evidenced by the fact that both Breen and Lipshitz have pursued further training as analytic therapists in London since leaving Sussex.

Two other smaller research networks also have contributed to the

Sussex center's prominence as a research setting in PCT. John Harrison and Philip Sarre have drawn on Kelly's theory and technique as a means of conceptualizing and studying the "images" persons have of their urban environments (Harrison & Sarre, 1971, 1975, 1976). Neil Warren's continued presence at Sussex until his death in 1982 was also important, not only because he went on to publish in PCT after his arrival there (Warren, 1966), but also because he introduced Nigel Lemon to the theory (Lemon & Warren, 1974). Lemon subsequently has produced some innovative grid work on the linguistic determinants of construct meaningfulness, using bilingual Tanzanian subjects (Lemon, 1975, 1976).

In sum, the volume of work performed at Sussex makes it the second most productive PCT research center in Great Britain, second only to the University of London. Although, like all successful clusters, Sussex has had some of its members hired away in recent years, the fact that Ryle and Lemon remain on the faculty would seem to guarantee its continued importance to the theory's growth in the U.K.

University of Edinburgh, 1965–1977. Although the University of Edinburgh has not been a high-producing research or training center in PCT, it has had some impact on the development of the theory in the U.K. chiefly because of its founder, George A. Foulds. Early in the center's existence, Foulds had collaborated on somewhat conventional studies of thought disorder employing grid techniques (Foulds, Hope, McPherson, & Mayo, 1967; McFayden & Foulds, 1972). Later, however, he became an outspoken critic of Kellyan theory, engaging in heated published debates with McCoy (1975) over PCT's value vis-a-vis psychoanalysis (Foulds, 1973, 1976). Unfortunately, the critical function served by the Scottish university ended with Foulds's death in 1977. But two students trained there—N. Heather and F. M. McPherson—subsequently established a vital research network at the University of Dundee.

University of Dundee, 1967–present. The University of Dundee was established as a research and training center in PCT upon McPherson's arrival from Edinburgh in 1967. Heather and Presley joined him at the Scottish university over the next two years, providing the critical mass necessary for major cluster-level development. In collaboration with Joan Draffan, Felicity Buckley, and others, the three produced a voluminous but well-focused literature in schizophrenic thought disorder over the next decade, concentrating on the differential breakdown of construct interrelationships in subsystems pertaining to "psychological" and "physical" construing (e.g., Heather, 1976, 1979; Heather, McPherson, & Sprent, 1978; McPherson, 1969, 1972; McPherson, Armstrong, & Heather, 1975; McPherson, Barden, & Buckley, 1970; McPherson, Bardon, Hay, & Kushner, 1970; McPherson, Blackburn, Draffan, & McFayden, 1973; McPherson & Buckley, 1970; McPherson, Buckley, & Draffan, 1971; Presley, 1969). While the Dundee group has produced work on other topics, e.g., group therapy (McPherson & Walton, 1970), its chief contribution has been the extensive and still active research program in schizophrenia.

University of Surrey, 1967–present. Phillida Salmon imported PCT to Surrey when she moved there in 1967 after completing her research with Bannister at Bexley Hospital. She worked there until 1970, when she left for brief posts at the London Institute of Psychiatry and Brunel before settling at U London's Institute of Education in 1973. During her years at Surrey, Salmon's interests began shifting from schizophrenia to developmental psychology (Salmon, 1969, 1970), a line of thinking which she continued after her departure (Salmon, 1976, 1979).

At about the time that Salmon left, D. V. Canter took a post at Surrey and was joined shortly thereafter by Stringer, who, like Salmon had been part of the active U London cluster. Although they published independently, both men had similar interests in applying personal construct psychology to problems of architectural and environmental perception (Canter, 1968, 1974; Stringer, 1974, 1975, 1976), and distinguished U Surrey from other PCT centers by their unique work in this area.

A final unique contribution by the Surrey group was represented by the work of A. E. Moss, who completed his degree in personality there in 1978. During the course of his studies he produced a pair of articles that utilized the work of Shakespeare to illustrate key concepts in Kellyan theory (Moss, 1974a, 1974b). In recent years attrition has reduced the size of the Surrey group, as Moss joined the priesthood and Stringer left to head the Department of Social Psychology at the University of Nijmegen in the Netherlands. Canter's ability to recruit additional students or colleagues with like interests will determine Surrey's future status as a significant center for PCT research.

University of Sheffield, 1968–present. In 1968, Dorothy Rowe, an Australian psychologist, moved to Sheffield and took a position at the

Wood Psychiatric Clinic, while simultaneously beginning work on her doctorate at the university. Rowe had been interested in discovering a research paradigm that would allow her to conduct idiographic studies that nonetheless were methodologically rigorous. Her discovery of the repertory grid that year seemed to provide precisely what she wanted. The following summer she attended a workshop sponsored by Bannister, Mair, Fransella, and Salmon—the "famous four"—and enthusiastically began employing the grid to assess changes in the depressive patients with whom she was working. She submitted the first paper resulting from the work (Rowe, 1969) to the *British Journal of Psychiatry* and, on the advice of a reviewer, contacted Slater at the U London for assistance in performing a more complex analysis of her results. That event was decisive; she and Slater became friends, and she consulted him on several subsequent single-case grid studies (Rowe, 1971a, 1971b, 1973a, 1973b, 1976; Rowe & Slater, 1976), both before and after her departure for Lincolnshire Hospital in 1972.

At the same time (1968–1971), a classmate of Rowe's at Sheffield, Steve Duck, was beginning his own program of research in PCT. Duck had encountered the theory the previous year in a class taught by Brian Little at Oxford and had gone on to do an undergraduate investigation of college-age friends using the grid. He carried this line of interest with him to U Sheffield, where he performed a series of studies on friendship development that gave rise to his first book (Duck, 1973).

Interestingly, Rowe and Duck—both graduate students—were the most active personal construct researchers to work at the U Sheffield setting. Two faculty members, however, also were involved in PCT investigations, though more peripherally. Peter Warr, a social psychologist, developed a series of studies bearing on factors affecting interpersonal judgments (Warr, 1971; Warr & Coffman, 1970; Warr & Jackson, 1977). The earlier two studies were noted by the construct theory community because of their relevance to the "meaningfulness" interpretation of extreme responding to bipolar construct scales (c.f. O'Donovan, 1965; Bonarius, 1971, 1977). D. A. Shapiro also made use of a form of grid technique in a study of group psychotherapy that he performed in conjunction with U London faculty (Caplan, Rohde, Shapiro, & Watson, 1975; Shapiro, Caplan, Rohde, & Watson, 1975). Both Shapiro and Warr have remained at U Sheffield, but its importance as a center for PCT work has declined in recent years.

University of Lancaster, 1973–present. Two years after completing his doctoral program at Sheffield, Duck assumed his present faculty position at the University of Lancaster's department of psychology. In collaboration with various colleagues and students in that setting, he has embarked upon one of the most energetic research programs to be conducted within PCT. His first concern was to validate a sequential, information-processing model of attraction and friendship development based on construct similarity between interactants at progressively deeper levels (Duck, 1973, 1975, 1977, Duck & Craig, 1977, 1978; Duck & Spencer, 1972). Currently, he is involved in a "downward extension" of his model to the acquaintance patterns of children and adolescents (Duck, Miell, & Gaebler, in press) and in an elaboration of his work to address friendship collapse as well as development (Duck & Allison, 1978; Duck & Miell, in press). Duck's work has helped foster a reorientation of the theory group toward more social concerns over the last five years (c.f. Stringer & Bannister, 1979).

Compared to American research and training centers, those in Great Britain are more firmly established. No American setting has graduated a number of high-producing theory group members to rival the University of London, and none has achieved the level of coordinated effort characteristic of the University of Dundee of the early to mid-1970s. No single center in the U.S. has developed a sustained program of research in PCT that has interfaced it significantly with another major theory, as has been accomplished at the University of Sussex. In summary, it appears that relative to their British counterparts, most American PCT centers (1) are more unstable, in that they typically involve fewer faculty and students, and (2) are more insular, seldom coordinating research with other centers or even between members of the network within that setting. As noted in the previous chapter, exceptions to this generalization are beginning to emerge. But on the whole, the institutionalization of PCT in the U.S. seems to be lagging behind that in the U.K., its historical head start notwithstanding. Parallel developments in rate of publication and coauthorship networking further a comparison of the two countries and will be considered below.

B. Publication Patterns in Great Britain

Once PCT had attracted a group of British adherents and secured an institutional foothold, particularly in the London area, production of intellectual materials by the group was rapid. This fact is dramatically borne out by the data in figure 4. In a span of less than twenty years,

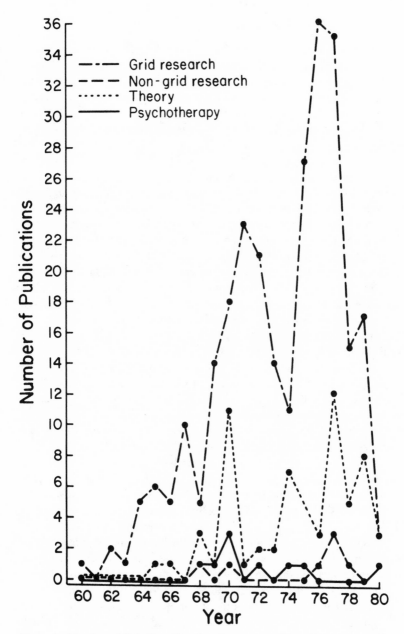

Figure 4. Number of British publications in construct theory by category and
year, 1960–1980.

British publications increased from the trickle of articles by Bannister and his co-workers in the early 1960s (averaging two annually from 1960 to 1965) to a relative flood of publications in the mid-1970s (averaging over thirty annually from 1973 to 1977). This publication explosion, which commenced in the late 1960s, suggests that Great Britain provided a more fertile intellectual environment for the growth of PCT than did the U.S., where the proliferation of research in the new style was less rapid.

Several intellectual developments may help account for this differential growth of the theory in the two countries. Among the most important of these was the construction, by Patrick Slater, of various principal components analyses of repertory grids, published in London in 1964. These computer-based analysis systems proved popular among clinicians as well as researchers. In the late 1960s, in what may have been one of the most significant sociological developments in the history of PCT, access to these programs was made available to all interested psychologists and psychiatrists in Great Britain by the Medical Research Council. As the sharp positive gradient for the number of grid research articles in figure 4 suggests, the availability of such programs unquestionably contributed to the widespread kindling of interest in the recently imported theory. This development was fueled further by the publication of Bannister and Mair's (1968) *Evaluation of Personal Constructs*, which summarized both Kelly's basic theory and the "state of the art" in grid methodology.[2]

In contrast to their American counterparts, who had displayed a concomitant interest in theory and research from the outset, British construct theorists preoccupied themselves primarily with empirical work during the first decade of PCT's existence in that country. Early theoretical contributions, e.g., to the study of schizophenic thought disorder (Bannister, 1960, 1962; Bannister & Fransella, 1965; Bannister & Salmon, 1966), were closely tethered to repertory grid methodology. This situation changed abruptly in 1970 when Bannister published *Perspectives in Personal Construct Theory*. The work was a compilation of more abstract and philosophical essays by prominent British and American theorists and represented the first book-length forum for original post-Kellyan thought contributing to or critical of PCT. Other similar volumes followed. In 1977, Bannister edited *New Perspectives*, which elaborated PCT's position on such issues as developmental psychology (O'Reilly, 1977; Ravenette, 1977; Salmon, 1977), emotion (Bannister,

1977; McCoy, 1977) and fundamental reappraisals of the theory itself (Radley, 1977). Two years later, Bannister joined Stringer in compiling an important volume that included several PCT forays into the realm of social psychology (Stringer & Bannister, 1979). The appearance of these books, along with the concurrent publication of numerous theoretical journal articles by British authors, firmly established the U.K. as a source of major conceptual as well as empirical contributions to PCT over the last decade.

As figure 4 depicts, the British have given even less attention to the topic of psychotherapy *per se* (independent of discussions of treatment-induced changes of client's grid scores) than have Americans, although there are some noteworthy exceptions (e.g., Fransella, 1972; Bannister, 1975). Similarly, nongrid empirical research by British investigators has been rare, and those few studies that have been conducted have appeared mainly in the late 1970s. The paucity of such studies is unfortunate, given that established investigators (e.g., Bannister & Agnew, 1977) have demonstrated the applicability of nongrid research designs to topics of considerable relevance to construct theorists.

Figure 5 displays the relative proportions of British literature in PCT which have appeared in learned journals as opposed to texts. As is true of the American literature, the publication of secondary materials in British construct theory (e.g., textbooks, collections of essays) did not become commonplace until the 1970s. In addition to those volumes mentioned above, several other books written or edited by British authors have spurred the international development of PCT over the last decade. In 1971, for example, Bannister and Fransella published *Inquiring Man*, the first textbook in PCT presenting the theory and the associated research at an introductory level. The paperback filled an important gap and quickly became the major undergraduate construct theory text in Great Britain. In the decade following its initial publication, the book sold over thirty thousand copies, mainly to undergraduate psychology students. Bannister and Fransella (1981, personal correspondence) believe that this level of student interest helped pressure academic psychology in Britain into providing more references to construct theory in the curriculum. The authors recently revised the book for reissuance in the U.S. and U.K., so that it seems destined to remain a significant gateway to the theory for third- and fourth-generation students as well. In 1977, Fransella and Bannister collaborated again to produce A *Manual for Repertory Grid Technique*, which has supplanted

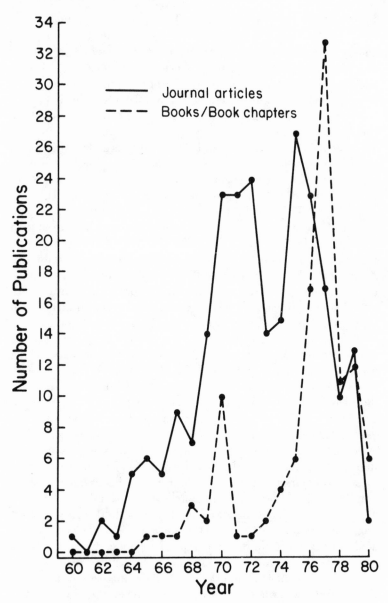

Figure 5. Number of British publications in construct theory by source and
    year, 1960–1980.

Bannister and Mair's earlier (1968) work as the primary methodological sourcebook in the field. Fransella followed this by her (1978) publication of selected papers based on presentations at the Second International Congress on PCT held the previous year in Oxford, England. Other authors outside the highly visible Bannister-Fransella-Mair "triumverate" also have published book-length contributions to the theory, although these have met with varying degrees of acceptance within "mainstream" PCT. For example, Duck's (1973) *Personal Relationships and Personal Constructs* represented one of the earliest systematic empirical applications of Kellyan thought to a clearly social psychological topic, friendship formation. Beyond Duck's own prolific writings (e.g., 1977, 1979), however, the uptake on his ideas by other construct theorists (e.g., Neimeyer & Neimeyer, 1977, 1981, 1983) has been slow. Ryle's (1975) highly original and provocative attempts to integrate PCT and object-relations work, at least at an empirical level, have been regarded with vague suspicion by purists in the PCT community. Slater's *Explorations of Intrapersonal Space* (1977), a volume of research articles employing grid technique, has excited somewhat more interest, both within the U.K. and elsewhere. In total, the outpouring of books and book chapters by British construct theorists has been so large that in recent years they have actually displaced professional journals as the primary publication outlet in the U.K. for work in the theory.

Figure 5 also displays the remarkable proliferation of PCT articles in British journals over the decade of the 1960s, to the point that they routinely appeared in such journals by 1970 (their apparent decline in recent years being largely artifactual). Not only was this increase in the number of journal articles more rapid than in the U.S. (cf. fig. 2), but British construct theorists also have been more successful in penetrating respected mainline journals in their own country. This is borne out by the data in table 5. In contrast to American PCT publication patterns, which show that less than 30 percent of PCT articles appear in APA publications, nearly 60 percent of British articles in the theory are published in journals sponsored by the British Psychological Society (BPS). Moreover, two of the top three most frequently utilized American journals are non-APA publications (cf. table 2), whereas *all three* of the most common outlets for PCT publications in the U.K. are sponsored by the BPS. In fact, only one of the five top PCT journals in Great Britain is not a BPS publication, the equally prestigious *British Journal of Psychiatry*. This suggests another important sociological difference in the status

Table 5

British journals in which personal construct theory articles
are published most frequently, 1960–1980.

Journal	# of articles	% of U.S. PCT articles
British Journal of Medical Psychology	58	16.5
British Journal of Social and Clinical Psychology	53	15.1
British Journal of Psychiatry	46	13.1
British Journal of Psychology	17	4.8
Bulletin of the British Psychological Society	9	2.6

Note: Fifty-nine percent of British journal articles in PCT appear in British
Psychological Society publications.

of the theory in the U.K. as opposed to the U.S. No American psychiatric journal has become a significant forum for PCT publication, and this seems to reflect the failure of American construct theorists to stimulate interest in their work among their medical colleagues.

Table 5 points up another striking difference in publication patterns in the two countries. In Great Britain, the top three journals collectively account for almost 45 percent of all published PCT articles; in the U.S., the top three journals account for only about 26 percent of published articles.

This discrepancy suggests the greater degree of diffusion in the American literature, where work in the theory appears sporadically in dozens of smaller specialty journals, rather than being concentrated in a few major ones. In contrast, construct theory research has established a secure and prominent niche in a few British journals having wide circulation. In part, this difference can be attributed to the smaller absolute number of journals in the U.K.: British construct theorists have

fewer publication outlets open to them than do their American counterparts. But this explanation alone fails to account for their relatively
greater success in publishing their work in respected journals, not to
mention the greater visibility of PCT generally within British academic
and clinical psychology and psychiatry. Incontrovertibly, there are
important sociological differences in the status of PCT in the U.K. and
U.S., and these will be examined in greater detail in a later chapter.

Table 6 partitions the number of British publications in PCT by
category and source. These data indicate that the British have displayed
somewhat greater reliance than have Americans on books as a forum for
their work (about one third of construct theory publications in the U.K.
have appeared in book form, in contrast to about one quarter in the
U.S.). Interestingly, the relative proportions of British and American
work devoted to grid research, nongrid research, theory, and psychotherapy remain the same (cf. table 3). However, British work is characterized even more strongly by repertory grid investigations, with over 75

Table 6
Number of British publications in personal construct theory
by category and source, 1960–1980.

	Books/ Chapters	Journal Articles	Total	%
Grid research	57	211	268	76
Nongrid research	5	3	8	2
Theory	45	21	66	19
Psychotherapy	4	5	9	3
Total	111	240	351	
Percentage	32	68		

Note: Total number of empirical publications (grid and nongrid) is 276, or 76%
of all published work. Of these, 268 (97%) utilize some form of grid.

percent of all publications falling into this category. In sharp contrast, only 2 percent of British work has been of the nongrid research variety. In other words, despite the impressive empirical base developed by construct theorists in the U.K., an incredible 97 percent of this work has relied upon a single set of closely related (grid) methodologies. This degree of technical devotion even exceeds that displayed by American construct theorists and leaves the theory group in a more vulnerable position than is necessary. The implications of this emphasis will be considered in a later section.

C. Coauthorship Networks in Great Britain

The coauthorship linkages among British members of the PCT theory group are depicted in figure 6. In comparison with significant contributors from the United States, those from Great Britain enter into fewer coauthor relationships: whereas 82 percent of American contributors collaborate on papers with each other or with others (e.g., students), only 64 percent of British contributors do so. The remainder simply do not coauthor, at least in their construct theoretical writings.

In spite of this greater preference for independent work, networks of British construct theorists display a greater degree of social structural cohesion than do American networks. This is reflected in the fact that seven British coauthor systems include three or more significant contributors, while only three such sizable networks exist in the U.S. This greater degree of "thickening" in the scientific communication structure in the U.K. may derive partly from geographical influences, since the concentration of theory group members in the London area would permit more frequent interchange of ideas and development of shared projects. In the U.S., in contrast, theory group members are scattered throughout dozens of cities hundreds and even thousands of miles apart.

The diversity of theoretical and empirical concerns that occupy British construct theorists is conveyed by a survey of the work of the more influential coauthor networks. Two networks that have been disproportionately productive relative to their small size are those gathered around Slater at St. George's Hospital Medical School in London and around Thomas at Brunel University's Center for Human Learning. As noted earlier, Slater's primary contribution to PCT has been methodological; he developed several popular methods for analyzing reper-

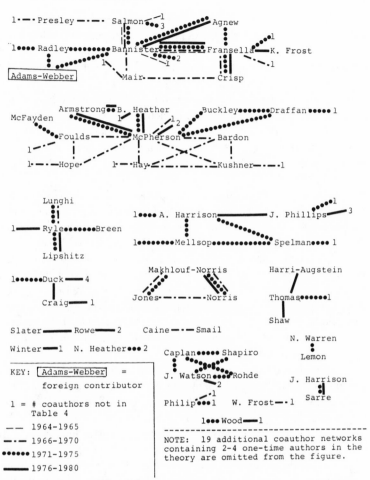

Figure 6. Coauthorship networks among British construct theorists, 1964–1980.

tory grid data (e.g., Slater, 1969, 1972) and more recently has edited a two-volume work comprising various applications of grid technique (Slater, 1976). Thomas and his colleagues similarly are known for their innovative methodological work, particularly in developing interactive computer programs for eliciting repertory grids from adult learners (e.g., Thomas & Shaw, 1977; Thomas et al., 1978).

Other small coauthor networks have concentrated more upon substantive research. Duck, for example, is orchestrating an ambitious research program at the University of Lancaster in adolescent friendship development, extending his earlier personal construct-based studies of the acquaintance process in adults (e.g., Duck, 1973, 1977). J. P. Watson and his colleagues have pioneered in applying grid methods to the study of psychotherapeutic group interaction (Watson, 1970; Caplan et al., 1975), and M. F. Makhlouf–Norris, H. G. Jones, and H. Norris have collaborated on a series of investigations of obsessional neurosis (Makhlouf et al., 1970; Makhlouf-Norris & Jones, 1971; Makhlouf-Norris & Norris, 1973).

The slightly larger coauthor group organized around Harrison has tended to follow the lead of the dominant British PCT network in studying schizophrenic and manic subjects using the methods devised by members of the larger group (Harrison & Phillips, 1979; Mellsop et al., 1971; Spelman et al., 1971). Somewhat more unconventional research has been pursued by Ryle and his associates, who have adapted grid technique to study conjoint marital therapy (e.g., Ryle & Breen, 1972a; Ryle & Lipshitz, 1975). Ryle also has championed the use of the repertory grid to measure psychodynamic formulations (Ryle, 1975; Ryle & Lipshitz, 1974), although this work has been received rather coolly by more orthodox construct theorists.

The second largest coauthor network in the U.K. has been orchestrated by McPherson in Scotland. Like the Harrison group, it has extended the pioneering efforts of the Bannister et al. network in exploring the dimensions of schizophrenic thought disorder. The chief contribution of the McPherson group has been an extensive line of research examining schizophrenics' use of "psychological" constructs (i.e., those pertaining to the personality or emotions of others) as opposed to "nonpsychological" constructs, and the relation of this preference to somatic, affective, and delusional symptomatology (e.g., McPherson, 1969, 1972; McPherson, Bardon, & Buckley, 1970; McPherson, Bardon, Hay, & Kushner, 1970; McPherson, Buckley, & Draffan, 1971). Given the convergence of interest between numbers of the two largest British groups, it may seem curious that no coauthorship effort has linked them. This is difficult to account for on purely intellectual grounds, although more recent work by Foulds, a member of the smaller group, is quite critical of Kellyan theory while apparently accepting the usefulness of its methodology (Foulds, 1973, 1976). As has been true of other work by authors employing grid technique outside the purview of the PCT proper (e.g., Bieri, Ryle, and Slater), such a position seems to be met with a mixed reaction on the part of mainline construct researchers.

The largest and most influential British cluster is gathered around Bannister and his principal coauthors, Fransella, Salmon, and Mair. Bannister inaugurated British work in the theory with his forays into the characteristics of schizophrenic thought (Bannister, 1960, 1962, 1963, 1965), a line of research in which he eventually was joined by Salmon (e.g., Bannister & Salmon, 1966), Fransella, and others (e.g., Bannister & Fransella, 1965, 1967; Bannister, Fransella, & Agnew, 1971; Bannister, Adams-Webber, Penn, & Radley, 1975). The group rapidly diversified beyond this substantive area, however, and produced the two most widely used manuals for grid technique (Bannister & Mair, 1968; Fransella & Bannister, 1977), as well as trenchant criticisms of traditional psychological research (Bannister & Fransella, 1971; Mair, 1970a, 1970b), and grid-based investigations of construct system change during psychotherapy (e.g., Fransella, 1972; Mair & Crisp, 1968).

Not only have members of this major British coauthor cluster produced a considerable amount of important original work, but they also have assumed the primary responsibility for collecting together major contributions of other construct theorists and publishing them in periodic volumes. To date, the network has produced four such edited volumes (Bannister, 1970, 1977; Fransella, 1978; Stringer & Bannister, 1979). It is interesting to note that of the sixty-six authors invited to contribute to these volumes, 24 percent are participants in the sponsoring coauthor network, 36 percent are major foreign authors not linked by coauthorship with the network, and the remainder are from small British clusters. *None* of the contributors to any of the volumes are from the larger British groups pivoting around McPherson, Ryle, or Harrison. Although this decision not to invite contributions from active researchers in other major networks may be explainable on intellectual grounds, it could also be construed sociologically as an attempt to "annex" smaller, unconnected networks while circumscribing the influence of the largest network's primary "competitors."

As was true of the American system, international coauthorship is rare on the British scene, occurring only once (linking Adams-Webber, now in Canada, with members of the primary British network who collaborated with him in investigating the structural properties of schizophrenic cognition in the early 1970s). To an even larger extent than was true in the U.S., the number of coauthorships among British theory group members increased dramatically over the decade of the 1960s, reaching its zenith in the period from 1971 to 1975. Since that time there has been a decline in the annual coauthorship rate; whether this will be a temporary phenomenon or an enduring trend remains to be determined.

5

PERSONAL CONSTRUCT THEORY OUTSIDE THE UNITED STATES AND GREAT BRITAIN

A. Research and Training Centers

Compared to the nearly one hundred twenty major figures in PCT working in the U.S. and U.K., the number of significant contributors in other countries is quite small, totaling less than two dozen (see table 7). Problems in obtaining reliable biographies on these contributors, combined with international differences in the degree-granting programs they pursued, makes it difficult to characterize their overall orientation. An examination of their publications, however, suggests that most of these figures were trained primarily in clinical psychology or personality, a general profile that corresponds roughly to that of most American and British theory group members. Comparatively fewer of these international contributors seem to hold degrees outside psychology, although some related disciplines (e.g., social work) are represented.

With the single exception of the four Canadian settings, centers for PCT work outside the U.S. and U.K. are widely distributed around the world and in one institution per country. Unlike major Anglo-American centers, most of them exist as bases of operation for only one or two (coauthoring) contributors; few have developed into full-blown networks of investigators that systematically train new (student) mem-

Table 7

Contributors to PCT: Outside the U.S. and U.K.

Adams-Webber, J. R.	du Preez, P.	Rathod, P.
Aran, M.	Kuusinen, J.	Reznikov, R.
Benjafield, J.	Lifshitz, M.	Schonecke, D.
Bonarius, H.	Liotti, G.	Schuffel, W.
Borgo, S.	Little, B.	Sibilia, L.
Catina, A.	Marcus, S.	Scott, W. A.
Cochran, L.	McCoy, M.	Warren, W.
Dingemans, P.	Miller, A.	Stones, M. J.
	Nystedt, L.	

bers. Each of the three most developed international centers, while still revolving around one central figure, nonetheless has been productive for a period of years in terms of both publication of intellectual materials and training of future theory group participants.

Brock University, Canada, 1970–present. The primary Canadian exponent of PCT is Jack Adams-Webber, who joined the psychology faculty at Brock University in 1970. Adams-Webber's first serious contact with the theory came in 1964, during his second year as a graduate student at Ohio State University. Up until that time he had been primarily involved in research in Rotter's social learning theory but had found it largely irrelevant to his clinical work. It was at that point that he was assigned Kelly as a clinical supervisor. Kelly's emphasis on the personal interpretations people employed to make sense of their experience struck Adams-Webber as "obviously important," as something that could viably apply to his own life and that of his clients (Adams-Webber, 1979, personal communication). Soon after, he became involved in the personal construct research team and began his dissertation under Kelly's supervision. When Kelly made the move to Brandeis in 1965, Adams-Webber accompanied him, and the two continued to work together until Kelly's unexpected death in 1967.

Following the receipt of his degree in 1968, Adams-Webber joined Bannister's research program in schizophrenia at Bexley Hospital in London. He worked with the Bexley group for the next two years, studying the assessment, simulation, and modification of thought disorder (c.f. Bannister, Adams-Webber, Penn, & Radley, 1975). Upon taking the position at Brock, he turned his attention to more social psychological topics, e.g., the impact of cognitive complexity upon interpersonal perception (Adams-Webber, 1970a, 1970b). Gradually he became involved in studying more formal aspects of construct system organization, such as the distribution of subject's judgments of other people and objects in terms of the contrasting poles of their personal dimensions (Adams-Webber, 1977). Brock has been strengthened as a training and research center by the joint sponsorship of this line of research by J. Benjafield, who chairs the department (Benjafield & Adams-Webber, 1976; Benjafield & Green, 1978). In addition, the Canadian center's newly formed link with members of the U Rochester group and particularly with Mancuso at SUNY Albany (see chap. 2) offers further possibilities for collaborative research and student involvement.

In recent years Adams-Webber has confirmed his status as a social and intellectual leader in the PCT community. His comprehensive review of personal construct research (Adams-Webber, 1979) is likely to serve as the best high-level introduction to post-Kellyan work in the theory for some years to come. Moreover, his role as the convener of the Fourth International Congress in PCT, which was held at Brock in the summer of 1981, establishes him as an important organizational leader as well. Finally, through his coeditorship with Mancuso of two edited volumes (Adams-Webber & Mancuso, 1983; Mancuso & Adams-Webber, 1982), he has helped stimulate innovative work in the theory, particularly in applied and cognitive experimental areas. In light of both Adams-Webber's productivity and the university's demonstrated receptivity to PCT, Brock appears destined to become still more important as a base for the theory group's development in the years ahead.

University of Haifa, Israel, 1973–1979. The only Israeli institution to sponsor PCT work was inaugurated in 1973, when Michaela Lifshitz began publishing research that utilized Kelly's theory and methodology. While still a student, Lifshitz spent time studying with Kelly at Ohio State shortly before he left for Brandeis. After assuming faculty status at the University of Haifa, she instituted an active program of research that involved a number of students and colleagues. To a greater extent than is true of most academicians, she focused her investigative efforts on significant psychosocial problems, particularly those arising from the structure of the modern Israeli family in the context of the country's nearly constant military conflict with its neighbors. Representative of this work are her studies of the impact of the father's death on the differentiation of social cognition in war-orphaned children (Lifshitz, 1974, 1975a, 1975b; Lifshitz & Ben-Tuvia, 1975), and of adolescent girls' identification with their fathers as one contributor to their sense of independence (Lifshitz, 1973, 1978). Together with her students she also has studied the adjustment of Kibbutz-raised children as a function of the cognitive compatibility of their parents (Lifshitz, Reznikov, & Aran, 1974). Unfortunately, Lifshitz died in 1979 at the height of her career. Since that time, Haifa has failed to produce any further published work in PCT. Like Ohio State, which also relied exclusively on the activity of a single faculty sponsor for its continuation, the life of the Israeli center seems to have ended with that of its leader.

University of Utrecht, the Netherlands, 1975–present. Han Bonarius, who was the first Dutch psychologist to promote PCT vigorously, initially came into contact with Kelly's ideas when they were presented in a personality course at the University of Leiden in 1961. Bonarius was immediately attracted to the theory because it seemed to offer an integration of both clinical and experimental approaches, which at that time were sharply divided in the Dutch psychological community. His newfound appreciation of the theory combined with his pre-existing desire to study further in the U.S., and in 1962 he went to Ohio State for two years to work with Kelly.

In the course of his stay at OSU, Bonarius wrote the first major review of research on personal constructs employing variants of repertory grid technique (Bonarius, 1965). After returning to the Netherlands, he took a post at the department of psychology of the University of Groningen, where he developed a line of research bearing on the interpretation of extreme responding on Likert-type scales anchored by the poles of personal or provided constructs (Bonarius, 1967a, 1971, 1977). This integrated series of studies is noteworthy because it exemplifies the Dutch school's strong concern for methodological and experimental rigor. At the same time, Bonarius wrote one of the rare discussions of Kelly's fixed-role therapy as applied to an actual case (1976a, 1970b), the first discussion of PCT therapy *per se* to be written by a non-British or non-American author.

Although Bonarius produced considerable research while at Groningen, the university itself did not develop into an important center for PCT work because none of its other faculty or students participated in the work enough to become significant contributors. Since assuming his present position at the Institute for Personality Studies at the University of Utrecht, however, Bonarius has cultivated a greater degree of participation in related research among students and colleagues. One student who became heavily involved in PCT research was Peter Dingemans, who began his graduate studies at Utrecht in 1974. The following year he took advantage of Utrecht's institutional tie with the University of Florida and spent a year there studying with Franz Epting and participating in the thanatological research program of the Florida group (see chap. 2). He returned to the Netherlands in 1976 and worked closely with Bonarius for two years before spending a second year at a major U.S. center, the University of Rochester. At Rochester, Dingemans collaborated with Cromwell and Space on various grid-based studies of schizophrenia and depression. He has continued to elaborate these interests (e.g., Dingemans, 1980; Dingemans, Space, & Cromwell, 1983) in his present joint faculty positions at the State University of Amsterdam's Department of Psychiatry and the University of Utrecht's Department of Clinical Psychology.

A third member of the Utrecht center to have a significant impact on its research program is Praveen Rathod, who joined Bonarius after completing his degree at the University of Amsterdam in 1976. Like Slater in England and Space in the U.S., Rathod's major contribution has been methodological. He has conducted extensive reliability studies of principal components analyses of grid data (Rathod, 1980) as well as completing a critical review of simple correlational and complex multivariate methods of grid analysis (Rathod, 1981). Rathod has suggested that grid researchers acquaint themselves with the work of scientists gathering comparable data in very different disciplinary contexts, e.g., numerical taxomony. His own work in interfacing grid techniques with the approaches of such diverse fields promises to yield analytic methods more sophisticated than those current in the PCT community.

With three faculty-level researchers, the University of Utrecht was among the most active and stable cluster of personal construct researchers on the European continent. In addition to its impressive research output, Utrecht also has been successful in training students in the theory, some of whom already have begun publishing relevant empirical and theoretical work. Freak Eland, for example, also spent a year (1976–1977) at the University of Florida and collaborated with both Epting and Bonarius in researching self-disclosure by means of Bonarius's Reptest Interaction Technique (Eland, Epting, & Bonarius,

1979). Another Utrecht student, Herman ten Kate, recently has produced a theoretical explication of Hinkle's theory of construct implications (ten Kate, 1981). As student involvement in the work of the cluster continues, Utrecht seems likely to consolidate its position as a prominent international research and training center (despite Rathod's departure from the center in 1983). This development is being reinforced by the tendency of other Dutch construct theorists (e.g., Roelf Takens at the Free University, Amsterdam) to maintain strong collegial ties to the Utrecht center while pursuing their own distinctive research (e.g., Takens, 1981).

As stated previously, several additional universities in a number of countries have produced PCT research, but these typically serve as bases of operation for only one or two theory group members. Those institutions represented by a coauthor pair will be discussed in section C below. A few other settings represented by only a single contributor deserve mention here, however, because of the likelihood of their developing into more important training or research centers in the future. Australia's Wollengong University, whose department of psychology is headed by Linda Viney, is one example. Viney has drawn upon PCT to construct a measure of "cognitive anxiety" (Viney & Westbrook, 1976), one of the more interesting nongrid PCT assessment techniques to be devised in recent years (Neimeyer & Neimeyer, 1981). Moreover, her studies of transitions in the lives of women (Viney, 1980) and the death concerns of seriously ill patients (Viney, 1984) are quite congruent with personal construct emphases on individuals' attribution of meaning. In addition, her new role as a regional coordinator for the Clearing House for Personal Construct Research (see chap. 6) should add to her importance as a representative of the theory in Australia. Also in Australia, William Warren at the University of Newcastle has initiated a series of studies of death orientation using modifications of grid technique (Warren & Parry, 1981). Taking a slightly different approach from the Florida cluster (Rigdon et al., 1979), Warren's work helps refine what is becoming an important focus for current PCT research. Finally, Mildred McCoy at the University of Hong Kong took advantage of her unique situation as a westerner in an oriental culture to conceptualize "culture shock" in PCT terms (McCoy, 1980). She also has produced an important elaboration of Kelly's treatment of emotion, linking a large range of positive and negative feelings to the validational fortunes of one's construct system (McCoy, 1977, 1981). Despite McCoy's recent departure for the University of Cincinnati, the Hong Kong center may grow in the future, since other faculty and students are becoming involved in related work (McCoy, 1979, personal communication). [1]

In summary, PCT has attained several institutional footholds outside the U.S. and Great Britain, although the number of theory group members working at such centers remains small by British or American standards. Nevertheless, three major research and training centers, all founded by persons who studied directly with Kelly, developed during the past decade. Two (at Brock and Utrecht universities) hold promise of still further growth in the future. In addition, other germinal centers (especially in Europe, Canada, and Australia) have begun to take shape quite recently. In light of these developments, it seems safe to predict that the next decade will witness the rapid expansion of PCT as a theory group of international dimensions.

B. Publication Patterns

Approximately 90 percent of the literature in PCT is Anglo-American in origin. Because of the relatively small number of publications in the theory coming from other sources, these have been considered collectively in the following analyses.

Figure 7 graphs the publication patterns for non-Anglo–American work in the theory, partitioned according to the same typology used in earlier chapters. Despite the smaller absolute number of publications and the shorter period over which PCT has developed outside the U.S. and U.K., the pattern of these publications bears striking resemblance to the graph of work by American theory-group members (cf. fig. 1). In both cases, personal construct literature was produced at an uneven rate in its early years and has been on a significant upsurge in the last decade, though the American increase predated the foreign by a few years. A roughly similar pattern was evidenced in the British literature (cf. fig. 4). Commonalities such as these argue for considering *international* factors in the development of the theory group, a task that will be attempted in the next chapter.

As was true of the work from the U.S. and U.K., the PCT literature from other countries consists primarily of empirical research utilizing the repertory grid. In fact, the higher rate of publication during the 1970s is almost entirely because of the popularization of grid methodology, with some increment in the rate of theory production also

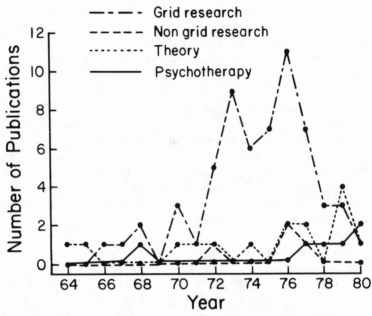

Figure 7.   Number of publications in construct theory outside Great Britain and
the U.S. by category and year, 1964–1980.

being discernable in the last few years. (The apparent decline in publications since 1978 is artifactual, resulting from delay in incorporating
references into retrieval sources.) With a few important exceptions
(e.g., Bonarius, 1970) the potential contribution of PCT to the practice
of psychotherapy has been ignored, and the applicability of nongrid
research designs to personal construct investigations has remained
largely unexplored. Thus, in these respects as well, the international
literature parallels the emphases apparent in Great Britain and the U.S.

The proportions of non–Anglo-American publications in PCT
appearing in journals and books are graphed in figure 8. Historically,
construct theorists in other countries have relied to a greater extent than
have those in the U.S. and U.K. upon scientific journals and bulletins
as a forum for their work. Until quite recently, the few book chapters in
PCT contributed by persons outside these two countries have appeared
in volumes organized by British or American editors (e.g., Bannister,
1970; Landfield, 1977). This situation is changing, however, as major

construct psychologists from other countries have begun to publish influential books of their own. Adams-Webber in Canada, for example, recently has written a volume entitled *Personal Construct Theory: Concepts and Applications* (1979). The work is a welcome one, updating as it does Bonarius's (1965) review and critique of PCT research and providing a useful supplement to Bannister and Fransella's less empirically oriented *Inquiring Man* (1971). Adams-Webber also has collaborated with Mancuso, an American, in co-editing a more theoretical volume of essays by theory group members teasing out the implications of each of Kelly's corollaries (Mancuso & Adams-Webber, 1982). It seems safe to predict that these two recent books will become important intellectual resources for construct theorists throughout the English-speaking community.

H. Bonarius recently has made a parallel contribution to the advancement of PCT in his home country, the Netherlands. His *Per-*

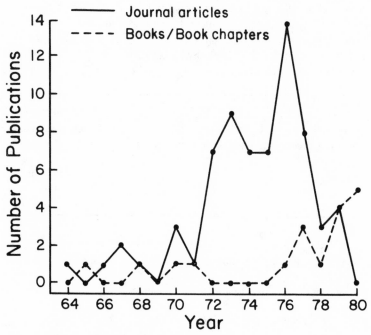

Figure 8. Number of publications in construct theory outside Great Britain and the U.S. by source and year, 1964–1980.

soonlijke Psychologie (1980) offers both a summary of the basic theory and a careful analysis of the international literature in the field, thereby making available for the first time a comprehensive introduction to PCT in a language other than English. As the sponsor of the Third International Congress, held in Breukelen, the Netherlands, in 1979, he also has co-edited a volume entitled *Personal Construct Psychology: Recent Advances in Theory and Practice* (Bonarius, Holland, & Rosenberg, 1981). The book contains a selection of the papers presented at the Dutch conference, and has been distributed to American, British, and continental European markets.

Table 8 lists the most frequently utilized journals for the publication of PCT material outside the U.S. and U.K. As this list indicates, these journals are scattered widely around the globe, providing a publication forum for both local and foreign authors. *Social Behavior and Personality*, for example, in spite of its being published in New Zealand, depends to a large degree upon its circulation in North America. It is not surprising, then, that it is a popular publication outlet for American construct theorists, who submit to it nearly as frequently as they do to some of the major U.S. journals (c.f. table 2). Similarly, *Psychotherapy and Psychosomatics*, despite its Swiss editorship, frequently publishes articles by British theory group members. The remaining journals tend

Table 8

Journals outside Great Britain and the U.S. in which personal construct theory articles are published most frequently, 1964–1980.

Journal	# of articles	% of PCT articles outside of U.S. & U.K.
Social Behavior and Personality (New Zealand)	13	15.1
Canadian Journal of Behavioral Science	7	8.1
Psychotherapy and Psychosomatics (Switzerland)	6	7.0
Scandanavian Journal of Psychology	5	5.8
Social Research Review (Israel)	3	3.5

to carry work by the major construct theorists in their respective countries (i.e., Adams-Webber in Canada, Nystedt in Scandanavia, Lifshitz in Israel). Despite the fact that none of these journals is a *consistent* publisher of work in the theory (in the way that several BPS journals are), these top five periodicals nonetheless collectively account for nearly 40 percent of the publication of PCT work outside the Anglo-American community. The remaining 60 percent is scattered throughout dozens of other publications, a pattern that more nearly approximates the dispersed U.S. literature than it does the more concentrated British work.

Finally, the total number of non-Anglo-American publications across time is presented in table 9, partitioned both by category and source. As a comparison of these data with those in tables 3 and 6 demonstrates, the publication patterns in the three major geographical regions are remarkably similar. In every case, grid research accounts for the bulk of the published work (63 percent to 76 percent), followed by

---

Table 9

Number of publications in personal construct theory outside Great Britain and the U.S. by category and source, 1964–1980.

	Books/ Chapters	Journal Articles	Total	%
Grid research	3	57	60	70
Nongrid research	0	4	4	5
Theory	11	5	16	18
Psychotherapy	4	2	6	7
Total	18	68	86	
Percentage	21	79		

Note: Total number of empirical publications (grid and nongrid) is 64, or 74% of all published work. Of these, 60 (94%) utilize some form of grid.

theoretical writings (18 percent to 23 percent), discussions of personal construct therapy (3 percent to 9 percent), and last, nongrid research (2 percent to 5 percent). Moreover, fully 94 percent of the empirical work conducted outside the U.S. and Great Britain has relied on some modification of the Role Construct Repertory Test, echoing the same over-reliance on a single method characteristic of Anglo-American work. In a theory having as large an international following as does PCT, it would seem reasonable to hope that the shortcomings of the literature issuing from one country would be compensated by the differing emphases of workers in other areas of the world. However, this has not been the case: the traditional neglect of therapeutic and nongrid work apparent in the theory's country of origin has been reflected with astonishing accuracy by the literature from other lands.

C. Coauthorship Networks

Something of the social-structural progress made by PCT abroad is reflected in the "map" of coauthorship linkages among significant contributors from around the world (see fig. 9). As the figure depicts, these networks tend to be rather loosely consolidated, seldom cohering into systems containing more than three major figures. On the other hand, 91 *percent* of the significant contributors outside Great Britain and the United States enter into these smaller coauthor groups; whereas only 82 percent and 64 percent of American and British contributors, respectively, do so. Although an explanation of this pattern must remain speculative on the basis of these data alone, it may be related to the relative position of PCT vis-à-vis the dominant psychologies in each of the three regions. Where the theory is less adequately institutionalized (i.e., outside Great Britain) theory group members seem to seek the tangible support for their work that can accompany close collaboration with one or two like-minded colleagues. Where the theory is less "embattled," more integrated into the national psychological scene (especially as in the U.K.), construct theorists may more easily work independently, supported by the general sense of respect accorded an accepted specialty.

For the sake of simplicity, only those eight countries represented by a *coauthoring contributor* (i.e., an individual publishing at least twice in PCT) are included in the figure, a format that obscures the fact that twenty-one different countries have produced published work in PCT. For the most part, these nations are concentrated in Western Eu-

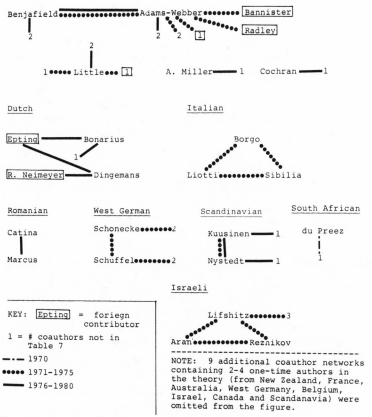

Figure 9. Coauthorship networks among construct theorists outside Great Britain and the U.S., 1970–1980.

rope, North America, and elsewhere in the English-speaking world, but Eastern European, African, and Oriental nations have begun to produce work in the theory as well (see chap. 6).

The only Middle Eastern coauthorship system to appear in the figure centers around Lifshitz and her Israeli collaborators, M. Aran and M. Reznikov, who have employed grid methodology to study the impact of parental similarity on the social maturity of their children in the unique family context of the kibbutz (e.g., Lifshitz, Reznikov, &

Aran, 1974). As noted in the previous section, Lifshitz also has written papers on other social/familial topics with students. The absence of further coauthorship since 1976 seems to reflect the demise of the once active network whose central figure died in 1979.

P. du Preez, at the University of Cape Town, South Africa, also has taken advantage of his unique social situation to study cultural and political phenomena indigenous to his region. Together with D. G. Ward (du Preez & Ward, 1970), he investigated the self-construction of traditional and modern members of the Xhosa tribe, focusing via grid technique on such variables as self-ideal discrepancy and construct permeability in the two groups. More recently, he has constructed a post-coding "dictionary" by means of which he has coded the shifting bipolar constructions used to frame political debates in the South African parliament (du Preez, 1972, 1975, 1979). Not only has this research yielded politically interesting results, but it has provided one of the most innovative nongrid PCT methodologies to emerge in recent years.

There are several active coauthorship clusters pursuing personal construct research on the European continent, most of which have become established only in the last ten years. J. Kuusinen (Jyvaskyla, Finland) and L. Nystedt (Stockholm, Sweden) have pursued a joint research program concentrating on the assessment of cognitive complexity on the basis of provided versus elicited constructs (Kuusinen & Nystedt, 1975). At the University of Ulm, in West Germany, W. Schuffel and O. W. Schoneke (1972) have employed grid techniques to study the effects of dynamic psychotherapy and to assess the cognitive structure of "hostile" cardiac patients. Two Romanian psychologists, A. Catina and S. Marcus, working at the Institute of Pedagogical and Psychological Research in Bucharest, have used personal construct methods to study appreciative style for forms of art (Catina & Marcus, 1976; Marcus & Catina, 1976). At the University of Rome, L. Sibilia, G. Liotti, S. Borgo, and V. Guidano (1972) have employed modified rep grids to determine the effective reinforcers experienced by alcoholics being treated by behavioral techniques. In addition, they have used grids to study Italian psychiatrists' perception of different models of treatment (Borgo, Liotti, Sibilia, & Guidano, 1972) and have reported that two (the medical and social) are construed to be in conflict. The influence of this network is likely to grow in the future, given the recent appearance of Guidano and Liotti's (1983) text integrating construct theory with other cognitive formulations.

The most active coauthorship system on the European mainland includes members of the Dutch school at the University of Utrecht. The preponderance of the published work of the group has been produced by single authors working independently (see section A above), but recent coauthorship ties between Dutch theory group members and the Florida group in the U.S. (Eland, Epting & Bonarius, 1979; Neimeyer & Dingemans, 1980; Neimeyer, Dingemans & Epting, 1977) have reinforced the collaborative links between the two nations.

Four Canadian research centers also have produced important work in PCT. L. R. Cochran, at the University of Newfoundland, has applied grid techniques to the study of such topics as impression formation (Cochran, 1976) and the evaluation of career alternatives (Cochran, 1977). At the University of New Brunswick, A. Miller has attempted to integrate PCT with conceptual systems theory (Miller, 1978), and has coauthored with a colleague a theoretical analysis of conceptual differentiation and integration (Miller & Wilson, 1979). B. R. Little, at Carleton University in Ottawa, has studied the differential interest people display in construing persons and nonhuman objects (Little, 1968; Little & Kane, 1974). The primary Canadian coauthorship network is linked around J. R. Adams-Webber and J. Benjafield at Brock University. Over the past decade the Brock group has produced collaborative studies evaluating the structural scores derived from different types of repertory grids (Benjafield & Adams-Webber, 1976; Benjafield & Green, 1978).

It is worth noting also that Adams-Webber's joint pursuit of the schizophrenia research with members of the British school (Bannister, Adams-Webber, Penn, & Radley, 1975) has established Canada's major coauthor link with foreign theory group members. Given its consistently high research output, it seems likely that the Brock-based coauthorship system will continue to expand in the future.

Despite the much later start among non-Anglo–American construct theorists in developing coauthor networks (the first such link was in 1970, in contrast to the early 1960s in the U.K. and the mid-1950s in the U.S.), the number of such ties seemed to peak in the first half of the 1970s, as it did in both of the major countries in which construct theorists work. Again, the existence of such international phenomena suggests the usefulness of examining worldwide trends to the theory group's evolution as a discipline, a topic to which we shall now turn.

6

THE INTERNATIONAL SYSTEM

A. International Publication Patterns

Thus far, observations on the sociohistorical evaluation of PCT have been confined to the *national* level, focusing on developments in the theory group *within* each of the three geographical regions where relevant work is being done. Although this level of analysis will prove crucial in determining the degree of maturity the discipline has attained (see chap. 7), it ignores equally important phenomena that become apparent only at the *international* level. Attending to the role of national interactions becomes all the more important when the theory group being studied is as multinational as construct theory (see table 10). But certain difficulties are inherent in this second level of analysis, since a construct theorist may be born in one country, be educated in another, be employed in a third, and publish or present papers in a fourth. Such cases are not hypothetical. Jack Adams-Webber, for example, was born in the U.S., received postgraduate training in Great Britain, assumed a university position in Canada, and presented a major paper at the Third International Congress held in the Netherlands. As H. Inhaber (1977) notes, isolating all of these geographical factors in order to evaluate the scientific community of a given country is probably impossible. None-

Table 10
Number of PCT articles published by senior authors of various
nationalities, 1954–1980.

Country	# of Articles	Country	# of Articles
Australia	3	Netherlands	8
Belgium	1	New Zealand	2
Canada	43	Poland	1
Finland	2	Romania	2
France	1	South Africa	5
Great Britain	226	Spain	1
Greece	1	Sweden	5
Hong Kong	1	United States	261
Israel	15	West Germany	5
Italy	2	Yugoslavia	1
Japan	1		

theless, a closer consideration of publication patterns within the discipline can provide a starting point for this analysis.

Although scientists usually publish primarily in the journals of their native lands, submitting occasional manuscripts to American or European international journals, the actual publication patterns of scientists from different countries vary widely. In fact, the distribution of publication locations for authors of any given nationality can serve as a rough gauge of the "scientific health" of that country.

If a nation's scientists hardly even publish in their own journals, it could indicate that they perceive them as weak. If they publish exclusively in their native land, it may indicate too much self-centeredness, and possible ignorance of work going on elsewhere. While it is difficult to place numerical values on the terms "too little" or "too much" publishing in one's native journals, it is likely that nations with a proper balance between national inputs and outputs of scientific knowledge lie somewhere between the two extremes. (Inhaber, 1977, p. 388).

Since the balance of native to foreign publications in a country's journals provides one index of the perceived status of that country's scientific periodicals in the PCT community, I have attempted to compare and contrast below the publication patterns of those countries producing the great majority of articles in the theory.

Figure 10 depicts the countries in which construct theorists from the five most productive nations publish. For each bar representing author nationality, the clear area on the *left* indicates the percentage of that nation's "output" (i.e., its total production of PCT material) that appears in that country's own journals. Publications in American and British periodicals by nonnatives are represented by the shaded areas on the graph, and the percentages of foreign publications outside the U.S. and U.K. are depicted by the clear areas to the *right* of the shaded areas.

The data in figure 10 indicate that 90 percent or more of the articles in PCT authored by British or American construct theorists are "self-publications" appearing in native journals. Interestingly, the "balance of (intellectual) trade" is roughly comparable for these two high-producing countries, with Britain exporting a slightly higher percentage of its work to the U.S. than it imports from American authors. Only 4 percent of the work from the U.S. and U.K. combined is published outside the Anglo-American community.

This picture contrasts sharply with that of the other countries represented in the figure. Canada provides the most striking departure from this pattern; less than 20 percent of the Canadian work in PCT is published in Canadian journals. The great bulk of the country's research instead is exported, principally to British and American outlets. In light of the fact that construct theoretical work has penetrated respected native publications (e.g., *Canadian Journal of Behavioral Science*), an explanation for this phenomenon cannot reside in a simple *inability* of Canadian theory group members to secure publications in their own journals. It seems more likely that Canadian journals, as a whole, may be perceived as "weaker" than their more prestigious British or American counterparts, making native publications less desireable.

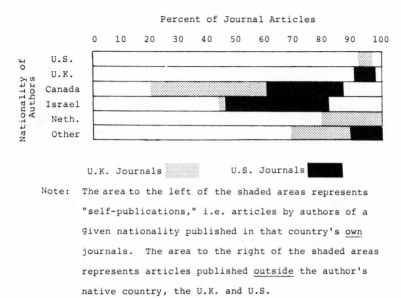

Figure 10. Where construct theorists from selected countries published, 1954–1980.

To a lesser extent, Israeli authors display a similar preference for foreign, and especially American publications. Just over 40 percent of the work produced in Israel stays in that country, while an additional 36 percent appears in U.S. publications alone. Dutch authors show less reliance on foreign journals. Eighty percent of Dutch research in PCT appears as "self-publications," with 20 percent being exported to journals in the U.K. The remaining countries having a smaller "scientific size" (based on their production of intellectual materials in PCT) publish over two-thirds of their work in native journals. The other 30+ percent, however, is exported to the U.S. and U.K. The high degree of British and American publishing for authors of all nationalities suggests that, at least within the disciplinary boundaries of PCT, the journals of these two countries are considered the most valued outlets.

A somewhat different perspective on these data is provided by figure 11. This figure depicts the origins of scientists *publishing within* selected countries (as distinct from the countries in which particular nationalities publish). Here, the clear area to the left of the shaded area

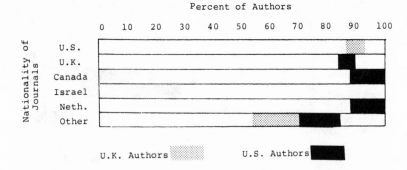

Note: The area to the left of the shaded areas represents
        the proportion of native construct theorists who
        publish in the journals of that country. The area
        to the right of the shaded areas represents the pro-
        portion of non-natives, non-Americans and non-British
        publishing in that country's journals.

Figure 11. Origin of PCT authors publishing in selected countries, 1954–
            1980.

represents the percentages of a particular country's journal articles in
PCT that are authored by natives. Shaded areas reflect the relative contributions to the literature of the selected countries accounted for by
non-native British and American authors. The area to the right of the
shaded areas indicates the percentage of articles authored by non-native
non-American, and non-British authors.

These data demonstrate that the literature in each of five countries most active in construct theory consists primarily of self-publications, i.e., works by members of that nation's own scientific community. (This is in no way inconsistent with figure 10, which showed a high
percentage of Canadian, Israeli, Dutch, and "Other" authors publishing in U.S. and U.K. journals, since collectively these still represent
only a small percentage of the work appearing in the journals of these
highly productive countries.) Israel exemplifies the limiting case of this
tendency toward self-publication: 100 percent of Israeli articles in PCT
are written by native authors. Whether this is a result of an editorial
policy (official or unofficial) to open Israeli journals only to natives, or

of a consistent avoidance of Israeli journals by theory group members working elsewhere, cannot be determined from these data alone.

The tendency toward self-publication in the major nations differs appreciably from the pattern displayed by "other" countries, nearly half of whose articles are written by foreign authors. Although relatively few British or American construct theorists export their research outside the Anglo-American community, such exports that do occur apparently find a receptive readership alongside the publications of native authors in "smaller" countries.

A clearer idea of the relative attractiveness of publishing in various countries can be gleaned from the information presented in table 11. That table compares the number of PCT articles authored by natives of a particular country with the number of PCT articles published by that country's journals. Only the U.S. and Great Britain are net importers of scientific papers in the theory (i.e., only they have a ratio greater than 1.0). The remaining countries export more articles than they import. This is especially true of Israel and Canada, which export the majority of their construct theoretical research without being compensated by receiving an equal number of publications from authors of other nations. Interestingly, the ratios of intellectual imports to exports in PCT reported for these five countries parallels quite closely the overall ratios

Table 11

Ratio of authors from, to authors publishing in,
selected countries, 1954–1980

Country	Authors from	Authors publishing in	Ratio of Column 3 to Column 2
U.S.	261	281	1.08
U.K.	226	241	1.07
Canada	43	9	.21
Israel	15	6	.40
Netherlands	8	7	.88

Note: As used here, *authors* refers to the first author of each article. Thus, one individual authoring three articles would be tallied as three *authors* on this table.

for them across *all* scientific disciplines (Inhaber, 1977). The single striking exception is the Netherlands, which has only a roughly "balanced" trade in PCT materials, despite its very strong reputation as the leading net importer and publisher of scientific work in other fields.

In summary, the major nations in the PCT community differ considerably in the degree to which native authors utilize their own, as opposed to foreign, journals for publication of their research. Not surprisingly, the vast majority of American and British investigators publish in native journals, though the relatively small percentage who publish elsewhere make a disproportionately large contribution to the literature of countries having a smaller "scientific size." Authors outside the Anglo-American community also seem to favor publishing in the journals of the two most active nations, perhaps because they regard the periodicals of their own land as relatively less influential, prestigious, or widely circulated to others in the theory group. Interestingly, as in other fields of science, their heavy intellectual exports to the scientifically more developed nations are not balanced by comparable numbers of imported articles by foreign authors. As a result of this imbalance of scientific trade, PCT may have a lower profile in nations like Canada and Israel than would be the case if native authors published more frequently in their own journals, or if British and American authors reciprocated by submitting occasional articles to the journals of these less active countries.

B. The Clearing House for Personal Construct Research

The previous section discusses certain significant differences—specifically in publication outlets—that characterize the development of PCT in selected countries. There are other developments on the international scene that also deserve attention and that to some extent serve to unify theory group members in various countries despite the differences between them. One such integrating factor is the Clearing House for Personal Construct Research.

During the heyday of Kelly's energetic social and intellectual leadership of the Ohio State center, he developed a substantial informal network of people interested in his work. Some of these persons were previous students, some colleagues at OSU, some professionals working elsewhere. A number of these individuals were interested in the new theory Kelly was engaged in building; others followed his work more out of an interest in Kelly as a person than out of excitement for his ideas. To maintain contact with this growing, heterogeneous group, Kelly gradually evolved a mailing roster, dubbed the "Magpie List," consisting of persons to whom he periodically mailed manuscripts and items of interest pertaining to his work.[1] This informal mechanism provided an important social and communicative link between members of the emerging theory group until Kelly's death in 1967.

In 1968, Al Landfield, one of Kelly's earliest and most active students in the theory, arrived at the idea of reviving and updating Kelly's mailing list as a means of maintaining contact among the scattered members of the young group. He corresponded with Leon Levy, Brendan Maher, and Don Bannister, all of whom had worked closely with Kelly, and received encouragement to undertake the task. That same year he wrote the one hundred twenty-five people on the old Magpie List and asked if they cared to remain on the mailing list of a clearing house for research in PCT. Fifty people (mostly personal friends of Kelly's) declined, and the Clearing House was inaugurated with a charter membership of seventy-five.

Under Landfield's editorship, the Clearing House has provided interested parties with a reasonably comprehensive annual bibliography of PCT, along with announcements of national and international conferences that might be of interest to the readers. In addition, it occasionally includes brief reviews of important books or articles in the field, announcements of the research involvements of new members, and updated rosters listing mailing addresses for its members.

Landfield edited and distributed the yearly mailing virtually single-handedly for the first ten years of its existence, receiving some help from Bannister in compiling European references for the bibliography. By 1972 the Clearing House had doubled in size to include one hundred fifty readers. This growth continued until 1977, when Landfield sought to eliminate from the list persons who were no longer interested in receiving the free mailing. This pared the list of recipients to less than two hundred, who formed the core of a revitalized membership. Since that date, the list has grown again to number approximately three hundred fifty individuals from twenty-one different countries (Landfield, 1981, personal communication).

Eventually the burgeoning membership combined with the ever-expanding number of bibliographic references to make the management of the service by a single individual impossible. For this reason,

Landfield invited Franz Epting to join him in coeditorship of the project in 1979. Finally, in 1980, the editors appointed an additional five "regional representatives" to assist in collecting and disseminating information in various parts of the world. Mildred McCoy (Hong Kong), Eric Button (Great Britain), Linda Viney (Australia), Han Bonarius (the Netherlands), and Jack Adams-Webber (Canada) assumed these positions, broadening the base of the Clearing House in order to serve better the needs of an expanding international community.

C. International Congresses on Personal Construct Psychology

A second, more recent development that has helped produce a sense of cohesiveness within the growing international theory group has been the convening of International Congresses on PCT biannually since 1975. Although the 1975–1976 Nebraska Symposium represented the first large-scale attempt to organize a major international conference devoted solely to PCT, it was foreshadowed by a smaller-scale effort orchestrated by Great Britain's Neil Warren over a decade earlier. Several members of the London theory group had been meeting for weekly "Kelly seminars" at Brunel University in the autumn of 1964. The group was a diverse one, comprising psychologists and psychiatrists at many levels of training, who were held together in large part by the social leadership of Don Bannister.[2] The seminars culminated in a "Symposium on the Theory and Methodology of George Kelly," featuring presentations by Warren, Bannister, Fransella, Ravenette, Mair, and Thelma Veness, as well as a special presentation by Kelly himself (later published in Maher, 1969). Twenty-six persons, all British, attended the presentations. Kelly's own participation made this first symposium "international," at least in spirit.

In October 1975, Landfield organized the 24th Nebraska Symposium on Motivation and was successful in attracting a number of prominent construct theorists from overseas to address the 143 participants. Although most of the participants in the conference were American, individuals from several states and five foreign countries attended, a fact that prompted its being referred to subsequently as the "First International Congress on Personal Construct Psychology." A valuable by-product of the symposium was the publication of the major addresses and a summary of audience discussion in the respected Nebraska Symposium series (Landfield, 1977). The congress thus contributed to both the social and intellectual momentum of the developing group.

The reception of the Nebraska conference was so enthusiastic that Fay Fransella began formulating the idea of convening a second congress in England two years later. She approached Finn Tschudi and Don Bannister with the notion and received encouragement for the plan. Under Fransella's organization, and with the assistance of Bannister and Mair, this second congress was held in July 1977 at Christ Church College in Oxford, England. It attracted two hundred registrants for the four-day residential convention. The trend toward increased international participation continued; the 30 percent of attenders who were non-British came from thirteen different countries, concentrated mainly in Europe, but including some as distant as Hong Kong. Unlike the Nebraska Symposium, the Oxford Congress was structured to include many smaller paper presentations by participants in addition to the major addresses to the entire group. Therefore, when Fransella decided to edit a volume (Fransella, 1978) containing contributions to the conference, she was able to include selected shorter papers as well as the texts of major presentations. This was important, since it provided a published forum for promising authors who were only beginning to establish their reputations as critical thinkers in the theory.

Following the success of the second congress, the "natural leaders" of the theory group (i.e., Fransella, Landfield, Bannister, Mair, Mancuso, Bonarius, Adams-Webber) met to plan the next meeting and elected to hold it in the Netherlands under the sponsorship of Bonarius. Thus, in July 1979, the Third International Congress convened on the grounds of the Nijenrode castle in Breukelen, Holland. One hundred and one persons attended, with national backgrounds as diverse as those in evidence at the previous Oxford Congress. In fact, the continental congress attracted registrants from Eastern European countries and South America, the first time that these nations had become involved in the expanding social communication network of the theory group. Like Fransella, Bonarius chose to publish a volume of selected papers by participants, and did so in collaboration with a British and American editor (Bonarius, Holland & Rosenberg, 1981).

The Fourth International Congress was held in August 1981 at Brock University in St. Catherines, Ontario, and was chaired by Jack Adams-Webber. James Mancuso as vice-chairman, along with Brian Hayden, and John Novak assisted with organization. As was true of both previous European meetings, the conference format included major presentations by international figures in the theory, supplemented by additional paper presentations by participants, a selection of which was published by Adams-Webber and Mancuso (1983). The location of the conference was important, since it helped encourage interest in the theory among the small but devoted network of Canadian adherents.

Finally, a Fifth International Congress was held in Boston, Massachusetts, in July 1983. Sponsored by Al Landfield and Franz Epting, with the support of Uriel Meshoulam, Greg Neimeyer, and Spencer McWilliams, the program offered a broader range of presentation formats than did previous congresses, including poster sessions and panel discussions in addition to the traditional plenary sessions and paper presentations. As with previous congresses, a selection of presentations will appear in an edited volume (Epting & Landfield, 1985).

In conclusion, the advent of international conferences in PCT since 1975 reflects the increasing maturity of the theory group and its growing multinational academic base, with attenders from over twenty nations. The congresses have provided both a kind of social-structural "cement" bonding professionals having common interests, and published materials (i.e., volumes of empirical and theoretical work) that have expanded the intellectual resources of specialty. It seems safe to predict that such biannual meetings will continue to serve these important ends in the future.

D. Other Developments

Certain other significant organizational developments in PCT deserve brief mention here, since they also indicate the level of social structural maturity of the theory group. For example, Epting in the United States has been instrumental in organizing meetings of persons interested in PCT at the last four annual conventions of the American Psychological Association. The meeting has not been devoted to presentations of formal papers but to updating construct theorists in North America on each other's work and informing them of professional programs (e.g., the international congresses) of potential interest. Though informal, this annual event is important, since it provides American and Canadian theory group members, who may work thousands of miles apart, the opportunity to interact on a regular basis.

A second noteworthy trend is that established professionals are seeking advanced training in personal construct theory, therapy, and research. Given the concentration of well-known construct theorists in the London area, that city has become the principle site for this continuing education. The demand for advanced work is not limited to members of the British community, however; Spencer McWilliams and Ed Hershgold from the U.S. are just two examples of academicians from other nations who recently have taken professional leave to pursue such training in the U.K.

In a related development, Fransella has announced the opening of the "Centre for Personal Construct Psychology, Therapy, and Counselling" in London. The center grew out of her efforts (detailed in Fransella, 1980) to teach advanced students and practitioners in the helping professions the implications of PCT for psychotherapy. The demand for this practical training has been so great that, in the span of three years, the center has expanded to offer a three-year, part-time sequence of courses in personal construct therapy, lectures, and residential workshops and has begun to provide individual and group treatment conducted from a personal construct perspective. This ambitious project seems especially important since the rich clinical implications of PCT have been insufficiently recognized, even by those who have familiarity with the theory (R. Neimeyer, 1980). The existence of an actual psychotherapy training site provides an excellent context in which PCT approaches to treatment can be systematized, tested, and empirically evaluated. Since August 1981, the Centre has published *Constructs*, a quarterly newsletter disseminating news of training opportunities and brief "thought pieces" of interest to an international readership.

The increasingly broad international base of the theory group is reflected in formation of a second organizational center for construct psychologists in Europe. Founded in Rome, The Italian Association for Personal Construct Psychology serves as the center for a nucleus of construct theory clinicians and researchers, including G. Chiari, M. L. Nuzzo, G. Gardener, F. Mancini, R. Lorenzini, S. Sassaroli, and A. Semerari. The group differentiated from the original Rome Center for Cognitive Psychotherapy, founded in 1979, whose focus continued to be more cognitive and developmental (cf. Guidano & Liotti) than construct theoretical. In spite of its newness, the Italian network has formed social ties with the British clusters through Bannister's visit in 1983 and has begun to write books and journal articles deriving from a personal construct orientation.

7

THE DISCIPLINARY DEVELOPMENT OF PCT: APPLICATION OF MULLINS'S MODEL

Summarizing the implications of his research into the evolution of scientific theories, Mullins (1973, p. 304) stated succinctly, "We can conclude that social support for intellectual developments is absolutely necessary if these developments are to prosper." Personal construct theory, as we have seen, was successful in mobilizing such social support both in its country of origin and abroad. Previous chapters have documented that the theory group identified with PCT exhibits all of the characteristics of other known cohesive scientific groups (Mullins, 1973, pp. 25, 26). These include:

1) A *theoretical break from its parent discipline*, developed by an intellectual leader, verbalized in a program statement, and supported by intellectual successes. Kelly, who remained the group's intellectual leader until his death, set out in his 1955 program statement the outlines of a theory that departed fundamentally from the predominately behavioral psychology of his day. Numerous intellectual successes (e.g., Bannister's research in thought disorder, Landfield's in psychotherapy) have supported and elaborated his original formulations.

2) *The emergence of a social organizational leader* who consciously seeks to develop the group by acquiring students, sponsoring symposia, and so forth. Kelly was the primary social as well as intellectual leader in the U.S. until 1967, at which time Landfield assumed

many of these responsibilities. Bannister, and later Fransella, Bonarius, and Adams-Webber performed parallel social organizational functions in other countries.

3) *The establishment of research and training centers*, sites of close interaction among group members, which also train the student apprentices necessary to carry out the group's research program. Ohio State University was the first such center in PCT. It was followed by a number of other American settings, as well as the universities of London, Sussex, Dundee, Utrecht, Brock, and others abroad.

4) *The publication of intellectual materials*, including a textbook in the orientation of the group, critical material, and secondary material. Construct theorists have published over a thousand books, book chapters, and journal articles since 1955,[1] including several important critical works (c.f. Bannister, 1970a, 1977a, 1984; Landfield, 1977) and textbooks at both the introductory (Bannister & Fransella, 1971) and advanced (Adams-Webber, 1979) levels.

Having considered in earlier chapters the several separate lines along which PCT has progressed (e.g., through publication, institutionalization, coauthorship), it remains for the present chapter to consider these collectively. Doing so should permit us both to trace the theory's progress through the various stages of Mullins's (1973) model, and to assess its current degree of maturity as a scientific discipline.

As the first chapter delineated, Mullins evaluates the developmental stage of a theory group by examining various indices of its scientific communication structure. Briefly, as a new theory group differentiates from its parent discipline, it progresses from a *normal* science stage characterized by few colleague, apprentice, and coauthor relations among group members to the *network* stage, when such relations begin to appear. Simultaneously, the group begins to rally around an exciting intellectual product and reaches an agreement on research style and direction, which is reflected in its program statement. Training and research centers begin to develop. The *cluster* stage often is ushered in by a "publication explosion," facilitated by the greater concentration of (coauthoring) faculty and students at a few major centers. Communication with scientists outside the cluster declines, and a social organizational leader emerges to promote the group's further development. As a result of this increased level of activity, the theory group becomes more visible to members of the parent discipline, who may come to regard it either as revolutionary or elite. Finally, as the group members are hired away from successful clusters, the theory emerges into the *specialty* stage. Although the output of the group may continue to grow as it produces texts, reviews, and further research, its communication structure gradually weakens as members re-establish ties with scientists in other fields. Institutionalizing the work of the group becomes a concern at this stage, with elite specialties gaining prominence through established journals and positions, and revolutionary specialties creating new ones. Eventually the communication pattern of the group begins to approximate that of normal science, as different factions of the group begin to elaborate their work in different directions.

A description of PCT's evolution in terms of Mullins's (1973) model follows.

A. Normal Stage, to 1955

Over the course of his clinical practice in the 1930s and 1940s, Kelly began piecing together a conception of personality and psychotherapy that later would be articulated as the psychology of personal constructs. In so doing, he incorporated significant themes from his own life experience into a theory that emphasized the capacity of individuals to construct unique patterns for perceiving and exploring their experiential world. These emphases placed him loosely among those psychologists identified with the "new look" in perception research (e.g., Bruner & Postman, 1949). Unlike others within this general framework, however, Kelly worked primarily from a clinical, rather than a social psychological vantage point, a factor that may have limited their collaboration. Thus, throughout the 1940s Kelly remained a relatively isolated figure (as he acknowledges in the preface to his 1955 work). As Mullins (1973) points out, this absence of significant collaborative relationships is characteristic of scientists participating in normal stage activity.

Soon after his appointment to the Ohio State faculty in 1946, Kelly began to set down the outlines of his theory in more explicit terms. He quickly attracted a handful of students (Landfield, Howard, Tyler, Bieri, Dugan, Crockett, Cromwell, Maher, Levy, Mischel, and Sechrest) who helped critique, elaborate, and test his early formulations. A significant social feature of this stage was the "Thursday Night Group," which provided both a forum for the discussion of construct theoretical ideas and a sense of *esprit de corps* for the participants in the small emerging theory group.

As figure 2 indicates, publication of intellectual materials by group members during the normal stage was quite limited, although a few pioneering articles did appear (e.g., Bieri, 1955; Howard & Kelly, 1954; Landfield, 1954). With the single exception of the Howard and Kelly paper, coauthorship was nonexistent. OSU remained the only research and training center in the theory throughout the stage; others who eventually were to become important participants in the emerging theory group (e.g., Rosenberg, Scott, Slater, Ward) were scattered throughout several universities in the U.S. and abroad, with no awareness of their converging interests.

B. Network stage, 1955–1966

This situation began to change in 1955 with the publication of Kelly's *magnum opus, The Psychology of Personal Constructs.* The appearance of this work marked the nascent theory group's transition into network status by providing both an explicit theory and suggestive program statement around which other psychologists could gather. As a result, Ohio State attracted nine additional students (Simmons and Blackman in the late 1950s; Adams-Webber, Suchman, Karst, Dolliver, Epting, Day, and Bodden in the early 1960s). While this number of group members nearly provided the critical mass necessary for the emergence of cluster-level activity, a stable and highly productive research group failed to form at OSU, principally because no other faculty sponsors beyond Kelly existed to catalyze its development. But the late OSU network was productive in a second, quite important sense. It trained many of the figures who would go on to establish active new networks in the U.S. and even provided apprenticeship experiences for international figures (Bannister, Bonarius, Lifshitz) who helped export PCT to their respective countries.

During the first half of the 1960s, the number of publications by American theory group members began to increase visibly. Bieri's (1955) research on cognitive complexity served as a paradigm for many of these studies, the bulk of which employed some variant of Kelly's (1955) repertory grid technique (see fig. 1). Small but active coauthor systems began forming around Bieri at Columbia, Crockett at Clark, and Landfield at Missouri. The Missouri center in particular increased in importance throughout the network stage, producing both important theoretical (e.g., Oliver & Landfield, 1962) and empirical (e.g., Landfield, 1971) work.

Clearly the single most significant communication link to be established between group members during this period resulted from Bannister's decision to send Kelly the results of his first PCT research early in 1958. The correspondence and face-to-face contacts that followed cemented the personal and professional relationships between the two men and fueled the rapid development of the theory group in Great Britain. Kelly's visit to the Maudesley in 1960 helped grant legitimacy to Bannister's efforts. Within a few years the U London network had grown to include Slater and Stringer as faculty participants, as well as several promising students (e.g., Mair, H. Norris, Smail, Fransella, and Wooster). Bannister (then at Bexley) continued to function as its intellectual and social leader. Publications resulting from joint research began to appear (fig. 5), and the coauthorship nexus binding Bannister, Salmon and Fransella began to take shape (fig. 6). By 1965 the U London network was poised on the verge of cluster-level development.

Meanwhile, pockets of interest in PCT were developing at other British universities. Brunel was particularly important in fostering the theory group's growth during the network stage. Warren's sponsorship of the first series of "Kelly lectures" eventuated in the 1964 Brunel Symposium, in which most of the prime movers of British PCT took part. Ryle, at U Sussex, simultaneously was planning his first work with grids to measure client change during therapy. Thus, although the U London network at mid-decade clearly overshadowed other British centers (as OSU overshadowed others in the U.S.), the seeds of later networks already were sown elsewhere throughout the country.

Intellectually, the network stage produced two major research programs. The first was a series of experiments by Bieri and others on cognitive complexity (reviewed by J. C. J. Bonarius, 1965). The second was that organized by Bannister at U London and Bexley Hospital concentrating on schizophrenic thought disorder. Although more recent, the Bannister (et al.) work became paradigmatic for later British work, much as Bieri's had provided an exemplar for American research.

C. Cluster Stage, 1966–1972

By 1966 the University of London network clearly had achieved cluster status. Fransella and Mair recently had graduated, and had taken faculty positions in the system alongside Stringer, Slater, and Norris. Capable students (e.g., Salmon, Watson, and Phillips) continued to enter the cluster. Bannister remained at Bexley through 1974, working closely with his U London colleagues. As Mullins's (1973) model would predict, the concentration of so much talent in a single locale apparently triggered a "publication explosion" on the British scene (see figs. 4, 5). The great majority of these publications consisted of repertory grid investigations of various topics. This is hardly surprising, since a major factor determining whether a theory group will enjoy such rapid elaboration is the availability of suitable technical and methodological resources (Mullins, 1973, p. 91). As we have seen, Slater's (1965) creation of computerized grid analysis packages, distributed both through the efforts of his students (especially Jane Chetwynd) and the Medical Research Council, laid the groundwork for the dramatic increase in grid research in the later 1960s. This development was further supported by the appearance of Bannister and Mair's (1968) *Evaluation of Personal Constructs*, which suggested research directions for subsequent investigations.

During this same period, PCT was gaining momentum in a number of other British universities. Ryle and Warren at Sussex were joined by Breen, A. Harrison, and J. Harrison. McPherson arrived at Dundee in 1967, and both Heather and Presley entered the Scottish network by 1969. Thomas, who had remained alone at Brunel throughout much of the 1960s, gained Salmon as a colleague and Lipshitz and Shaw as students in the early 1970s. It is interesting that *all four* of the major British research and training centers in PCT reached their highwater mark about 1972, after which time they experienced a slow attrition as faculty began to be hired away by other institutions.

British construct theorists engaged in a great deal of social organizational activity during the cluster years, thereby becoming highly visible in the British psychological community. This activity proceeded along several fronts. The U London team (i.e., Bannister, Fransella, Mair, and Salmon) sponsored a number of miniconferences on Kellyan theory as well as workshops in grid technique. Just as important, Bannister's witty but incisive criticism of Eysenck's brand of nomothetic psychology became a regular feature of annual British Psychological Society meetings. While more conservative members of the young theory group sometimes lamented Bannister's polemics on these occasions, these debates nonetheless served an important function, attracting to the theory scarce resources, i.e., students, who identified with PCT's iconoclastic claims (Holland, 1979, personal communication).

The intellectual materials produced in the U.K. during the cluster stage began to diversify somewhat in content but retained the study of schizophrenic thought disorder as the major focus (one shared by both the U London and U Dundee centers). The concentration of sizable research teams on such focal topics produced extensive coauthorship systems, which continued to increase in number through the early 1970s (see fig. 6). As communication within the theory group became more ingrown, fewer references were made to work conducted in other fields (see chap. 8). In short, British PCT from 1966 to 1972 could be characterized as a very cohesive and empirically focused intellectual community that acted on both the social and cognitive levels (Mulkay, 1979, p. 89) to establish itself as a credible alternative to the more behavioristic mode of theorizing characteristic of its parent discipline. Its success in this effort can be assessed when its status in the specialty stage is considered below.

But what was happening in the American PCT community during this period of social and intellectual ferment in Great Britain? In a word, the answer is "less." The Ohio State network disintegrated with Kelly's departure for Brandeis in 1966, surviving only long enough for the youngest of Kelly's students (Epting, Day, and Bodden) to graduate. At first, Kelly's move to Brandeis seemed to be an auspicious development for the theory group. For the first time, he became part of a strongly supportive department. Both Maher, one of Kelly's former and most trusted students, and Maslow, a leading representative of the humanistic "third force" in American psychology, were available as faculty colleagues. Kelly brought with him a mature apprentice in the person of Adams-Webber, a methodologically sophisticated graduate student who could have helped establish an active PCT research program. Unfortunately, Kelly died before Brandeis's promise as a training and research center could be realized, and the university survived as an institutional setting for work in the theory only until Adams-Webber's graduation.

Having lost its intellectual and social leader as well as its most promising center for development, the American theory group attemped to regroup under the leadership of Landfield, then at the University of Missouri. To an impressive degree, Landfield was able to foster greater communicative cohesion within the expanding international group with the creation of the Clearing House for Personal Construct Research in 1968 (see chap. 6). In addition, he successfully orchestrated a major research program in psychotherapy outcome at the Missouri center (Landfield, 1971), thereby providing an important measure of intellectual leadership in the field. But Landfield's task ultimately was an impossible one. U Missouri was not the hotbed of PCT in the U.S. that U London was in the U.K. The only other construct theorist on the psychology faculty was Dolliver, and his theoretical differences (see chap. 3) with Landfield precluded a close collegial tie between the two men. Landfield's only significant faculty collaborator was Oliver in the department of philosophy, and he retired in 1971. Thus, unlike Bannister in Great Britain, Landfield confronted his job primarily alone.

A more significant impediment to the development of a British-style cohesiveness among American theory group members was the institutional structure of the group nationwide. In Great Britain by 1972, over 53 percent of theory group members were aligned with one of the four major clusters (London, Sussex, Brunel, or Dundee). The remainder were distributed through an additional twenty-one institutions, but these were confined to a relatively compact geographical area. Moreover, the great majority of British construct theorists were working in clinical psychology, thereby increasing the likelihood that they would be acquainted with one another's work. None of these favorable social features characterized PCT in the United States. The forty-two significant American contributors at that time were scattered among thirty-eight institutions located from southern California to New York, and from Washington state to Florida. *Collectively*, the top four U.S. networks (Missouri, Florida, SUNY-Albany, and Temple University) accounted for only nine persons, or 21 percent of U.S. theory group participants (U London alone had twelve). In addition, the fact that American PCT lacked a clear research focus (being split among clinical, social-psychological, and personality fields) further aggravated communication problems. The intellectual output of the group continued to climb, but much more gradually than the exploding British literature for the same period (compare figs. 2, 5). Finally, although the coauthorship system in the U.S. kept expanding throughout the early 1970s, it remained more fractionated than its British counterpart (compare tables 3, 6).

In short, while the British theory group had firmly attained cluster status by the early 1970s, the *U.S. group remained in early network-level development.* An appreciation of this differential rate of social-structural progress in the two major branches of the PCT community is essential to understanding the dilemmas that presently face the theory group as a whole. We will return to this theme after examining PCT's evolution into specialty status.

D. Specialty Stage, 1972–present

Having attained their peak membership, most of the large British networks began a perceptible decline after 1972. This process of attrition was quite evident at U London, whose PCT group dwindled from twelve to five over the decade of the 1970s. Between 1972 and 1975 alone, Radley, Applebee, and Poole graduated and left, and Mair, Stringer, and Norris moved on to take faculty positions elsewhere. A similar decline took place at U Sussex, though it began a few years later. The thinning of the Brunel center was quite abrupt; it peaked in membership in 1972, only to be reduced to Thomas and a single promising student three years later. As Mullins (1972) observes, the loss of its productive members to other institutions is the predictable—if ironic— price that the active cluster pays for its success.

In contrast, U.S. research and training centers during the same period began to grow in both membership and intellectual output. The University of Florida PCT network expanded throughout the 1970s by recruiting numerous undergraduate (Leitner, R. Neimeyer, and G. Neimeyer) and graduate students (Wilkins, Krieger, Rainey, and Rigdon). Its development was facilitated further by the participation of Dutch exchange students (Dingemans and Eland) in its research program from 1975 to 1977. The early to mid-1970s also witnessed the emergence of the U Kansas network, whose pivotal figures (Crockett, Press, and Delia) began to investigate a range of topics bearing on social perception and communication. At the same time, Landfield's move from Missouri in 1972 inaugurated U Nebraska as a PCT research center. Within a few years, it also began building a reputation as a training center, attracting both Leitner and R. Neimeyer from the Florida network to pursue graduate studies. By the late 1970s a number of other institutions (e.g., U Rochester, Notre Dame, SUNY-Albany) began to establish themselves as active research networks as well. Thus, just as local clusters of colleagues and students were beginning to break up in Great Britain, network ties among theory group members were beginning to thicken in the U.S.

But how are we to account for the movement of the British theory group into and *out of* the cluster stage, while its American counterpart was only inching toward active *network* status? According to Mullins (1981, personal communication), a partial answer lies in the relative degree of *institutionalization* achieved by PCT in the two nations. By the early 1970s, PCT in the U.K. was firmly ensconsed as the "loyal opposition" to mainstream British psychology. Thus, while construct theorists continued to take issue with the "mechanism" and "determinism" characteristic of their parent discipline, they nonetheless championed a methodology—repertory grid technique—that seemed to fit comfortably within the highly quantitative research paradigm endorsed by most British psychologists. It is true that PCT was perceived as a deviant orientation by many English researchers, especially in the early years. But most practicing construct theorists also served as allies against the larger threat to traditional logical-empiricist values represented by the infusion into Britain of the considerably "looser" phenomenological tradition in the 1960s. This capacity of British PCT to coexist with more conventional theoretical schools enabled the theory group successfully to institutionalize its work beginning in the early 1970s. This process was foreshadowed by the publication of the Bannister and Mair program statement in 1968 and was furthered by the appearance of additional secondary materials (e.g., Bannister's edited collection of essays in 1970; Bannister and Fransella's 1971 text, Fransella's 1972 research in psychotherapy) over the next few years. At the same time, PCT articles began to share space with traditional studies in the most respected British journals (see table 5), as construct theorists began to assume prominent positions on their editorial boards. The *British Journal of Medical Psychology,* for example, has been edited or coedited by contributors to PCT (Crisp and then Watson) since 1972. In addition, several well-known theory group members (e.g., Mair, Fransella, and Ryle) have served on its Board of Assessors. In a parallel development, construct theorists have begun ascending to positions of prominence in the clinical division of the BPS. Thus, although it retained something of a "maverick" reputation within the parent discipline, PCT had established a place for itself in the literature, curriculum, and political power structure of British psychology. With institutionalization of its position well under way, the theory group in the U.K. could afford to relinquish some of the powerful communication, colleague, and coauthor ties (see fig. 6) that had made it such a tight-knit intellectual community during the cluster phase.

    Not surprisingly, the work of institutionalization proceeded more slowly within the less cohesive American theory group. On the meta-theoretical level, the affinity between PCT and "humanistic" personality theories (Epting, 1980, personal communication) raised suspicion among behavioristic and empiricistic psychologists, thereby minimizing the theory's chance of establishing itself in the mainstream American journals they edited. Kelly himself passed up a chance to open this important publication forum to PCT-oriented research when he declined the editorship of the powerful *Journal of Abnormal and Social Psychology* (Bannister, 1979, personal communication).[2] The failure of American construct theorists to institutionalize their work in established journals is documented in table 2.

In other respects as well, PCT has been slower to establish a niche for itself within the American psychological community. For example, most active American construct theorists have preferred to remain uninvolved in the explicitly political activities of the American Psychological Association, Kelly's earlier chairmanship of the APA's consulting and clinical divisions notwithstanding. The U.S. production of secondary materials, such as edited books, also has lagged behind the British, with the first such works appearing only recently (Landfield, 1977; Landfield & Leitner, 1980; Epting & Neimeyer, 1984). Consequently, at a time when the British theory group no longer required a tightened communication structure in order to ensure its survival, the more slowly progressing institutionalization of American work continued to necessitate the development of close network ties if the theory group was to remain viable.

In terms of Mullins's (1973) model, these developments suggest that PCT has come to be regarded by British psychologists as an *elite* specialty, while it continues to be seen as more *revolutionary* in the U.S. These terms must be used in a relative sense in this context, because 1) the reaction of the parent discipline to the British theory group has its ambivalent aspects (Fransella, 1978a), and 2) PCT is only just now beginning to attract widespread attention in the U.S. (Davisson, 1978), hence the American reaction is less well defined. But it seems clear that British construct theorists are granted at least a modicum of respect in their home country, if only as the primary guardians of an attractive and somewhat esoteric (grid) methodology. This being the case, PCT could institutionalize in the U.K. by making a "takeover bid" for established journals and positions (see Fransella, 1978a). ·

In the U.S., on the other hand, construct theory was more identified with a suspiciously "humanistic" orientation than with any methodological expertise. At best, the American theory group was less socially
and intellectually visible to its parent discipline than its British counterpart: while the two countries have produced about the same absolute
number of publications and significant contributors, these were greatly
diluted in the much larger American psychological community. The net
result was that the U.S. group was forced to institutionalize its work more
slowly.

Finally, as PCT attained specialty status in the early 1970s, contributions to the theory from persons outside the U.K. and U.S. began to
appear in significant numbers. This was evidenced by the formation of
three very active research and training networks (at Utrecht, Brock, and
Haifa), and by a fourfold increase in international publications in 1972
(see fig. 8), echoing the concomitant explosion in the British literature.
In its communication structure the international scene mirrors that in
the U.S.: most theory group members are linked by colleague or
coauthor ties to only a few others. Nonetheless, non-British and American authors have produced two secondary works of major importance—
Adams-Webber's (1979) and H. Bonarius's (1980) texts—which should
contribute to PCT's attempts to institutionalize its work on a worldwide scale.

The intellectual output of the theory group as a whole has diversified considerably throughout the specialty stage, growing outward
from its home bases in cognitive complexity and thought disorder into
such realms as environmental construing, friendship formation, and
politics (Adams-Webber, 1979). This trend toward differentiation of interests is particularly apparent among noted British theorists (e.g., Mair,
Radley), who have increasingly turned toward integrating their work
with compatible philosophical traditions such as symbolic interactionism and European phenomenology.

Socially, the specialty stage has produced one development of
overriding importance: the regular biannual convening of international
congresses on PCT since 1975. By rotating the responsibility for such
conferences to social organizational leaders in various countries, construct theorists have fostered the sort of coordination of activities that is
vital to the success of large, multiple-cluster theory groups (Mullins,
1973).

E. A Forward Glance

Having assessed personal construct theory's progress through the various stages of disciplinary maturity, it is difficult to resist the opportunity to engage in a bit of "social forecasting." In anticipating the directions in which the theory group is likely to move, I will keep my remarks here brief, since some of these same themes will be explored in greater detail in the following chapter.

First, I would expect PCT in Great Britain to further institutionalize its work through the publication of secondary materials such as edited books of essays, texts, and critical reviews. This prediction appears to be a safe one, given the regular production of such works throughout the past decade (e.g., Bannister & Fransella, 1971; Fransella, 1978; Ryle, 1975; Stringer & Bannister, 1979). But the character of this material is likely to change in the future, as new intellectual leaders emerge who will integrate PCT with other schools of thought, thereby reducing its distinctiveness as a theoretical position. The theory should continue to be well represented on important editorial boards and in prominent political positions as the British group further consolidates its specialty status. Group cohesiveness, as indexed by colleague and coauthor ties, may decline as members migrate from a few major centers to several smaller ones. In the past, the lack of common training in PCT has necessitated the close student-teacher basis of the group. As the theory is included in more coursework in clinical, personality, and social psychology, the coming years may witness a mushrooming in the number of students who enter the specialty. This may produce an upsurge in the group's intellectual output for a time, but the number of publications eventually should plateau as the new (and less theoretically committed) generation of researchers channels its efforts into other fields of inquiry as well.

The situation of PCT in the U.S. is more equivocal. At present, the theory group shows signs of both precluster and specialty-level development. On the one hand, most research and training centers in this country remain very small; no one of them has had sufficient prominence to become an organizational nucleus for the American group as a whole. On the other hand, major secondary works (usually associated with mature specialties) have begun to appear (e.g., Landfield, 1977; Landfield & Leitner, 1980).[3] Such discontinuities may represent a tendency on the part of the American group to "jump the gun" by moving from network status into a kind of specialty stage without going through a real cluster stage. If so, the long-range results could prove deleterious to the theory's development, since few theory groups can survive the diffusion of effort characteristic of the mature specialty without first consolidating their communication and power base during clusterhood. The attempt to sidestep this necessity, for example, seems to have played a crucial role in the demise of sociology's small group theory (Mullins, 1973; pp. 118–119).

If the American group is in fact at this choice point—and I believe it is—then it can move in one of at least two directions. First, it could choose to pursue further specialty development by continuing to publish in dozens of journals, establishing only very small, local research networks, trusting that the existing literature will attract and hold the interest of promising students, and so forth. If the U.S. theory group takes this course, then it can continue to rely upon its better institutionalized British counterpart for support, e.g., by exporting more of its work to prestigious BPS journals (see chap. 6). Indeed, there are aspects of this course of development that are attractive, perhaps even important. For example, a number of U.S. construct theorists (e.g., Crockett, 1980, personal communication) are becoming interested in opening a dialogue between PCT and cognitive theories arising from within experimental psychology, the sort of interdisciplinary exploration that usually typifies members of established specialties. But there are also disadvantages; in particular, it seems improbable that any unique contribution PCT has to make to American psychology will be recognized and elaborated without a greater degree of intellectual focus and social promotion than "leap-frogging" to a specialty status is likely to involve.

The second, and in my mind sounder, direction that the U.S. group could pursue would be to take the time (perhaps four to eight years; Mullins, 1973) required to establish a few active clusters. This need not imply that all activities associated with specialty-level development (e.g., the publication of edited books) should be postponed until such clusters have matured. But it does imply that the organizational development of the group be given equal priority by concentrating more upon the recruitment of interested students and faculty to active networks, carving out a niche for PCT within the political structure of the APA, and so on. Such efforts could increase the intellectual as well as social visibility of the theory group within the parent discipline; for instance, by facilitating the establishment of larger-scale research programs coordinated by multiple investigators within the same center. At present, the University of Florida appears to be the most propitious spot for cluster-level development. The 1981 addition of Greg Neimeyer to the pre-existing network could trigger a rapid expansion of Florida's research program, especially if student participation in the network's activities remains high. Crockett at Kansas, Landfield at Nebraska, Delia at Illinois, and Mancuso at Albany also could spark eventual cluster development, given their status as established and active researchers.

Finally, the future of PCT in countries outside the U.S. and Great Britain remains to be considered. International differences make a single, blanket prediction very difficult. Generally, however, I would expect that most non-American and non-British construct theorists would continue to rely upon the larger two PCT communities for secondary materials and publication outlets (see chap. 6), while making the unique individual contributions that their intellectual "distance" from the major lines of research enables them to pursue (e.g., du Preez, 1979; Viney & Westbrook, 1976). Where local network thickenings exist (e.g., in Canada and the Netherlands), the activities of such theory groups would more closely approximate the Anglo-American model. The production of major texts and edited works by Adams-Webber (1979) and Bonarius (1980; Bonarius et al., 1981) accords with this conclusion.

F. An Evaluation of Mullins's Model

My primary aim in the present study has been to illuminate the sociohistorical development of PCT, and Mullins's stage theory has been my most important conceptual tool for doing so. But it seems appropriate to step back for a moment from this task to consider the usefulness of the model itself. How adequate a description of construct theory's progress did Mullins's system provide?

In general, the model worked remarkably well. PCT originated in a well-defined normal stage characterized by sparse research output and a very low degree of social structural cohesiveness, just as Mullins would predict. The shift of the young theory group into network status was clearly signaled by the publication of Kelly's *Psychology of Personal Constructs* in 1955. Transitions into later stages were less precise and were more easily gauged by social indicators (e.g., the emergence of intellectual leaders, the recruitment of personnel to training and research centers) than by theoretically concomitant intellectual properties (e.g., the appearance of a program statement or critical material). Even so, intellectual developments seldom departed in any marked way from the model and often corresponded quite well with related social trends (e.g., the initiation of cluster level activity in the U.K. was followed closely by a clearly discernable publication explosion). Where the reality of PCT's evolution varied from the expected pattern, these events usually were easily interpretable. For example, the unusual length and comprehensiveness of Kelly's 1955 work allowed it to function not only as the theory group's first success but also as a program statement for later researchers. Ordinarily, such statements do not appear until later in the network or early cluster stages.

Network thickening was found to appear in all those countries whose contribution to PCT has been most substantial. Moreover, the temporal association between such thickening and the production of important secondary materials supports Mullins's (1973) fundamental contention that good ideas, in order to develop, require social support. Minor deviations from the model were apparent in the exact size networks would be expected to reach before such materials would appear: Landfield in the U.S. and Adams-Webber in Canada both produced secondary work before American or Canadian networks had achieved full cluster status. Even this variation is understandable, however, since their books incorporate work done by the social-structurally more mature British theory group.

In accordance with the model, cluster development in Great Britain was accompanied by an increase in the group's social visibility as well as its intellectual output. The appearance of highly productive student and coauthor groups during this stage also matches predictions. As the theory group in the U.K. began to institutionalize its work (e.g., by taking over positions in major journals and the BPS, and by publishing texts), members of the larger clusters began to take positions elsewhere, as Mullins would hypothesize. The only significant departure from Mullins's original (1972) model in the specialty stage is that PCT's intellectual leaders have continued to work within the specialty they helped found, whereas in the physical and biological sciences they often move on to cultivate advances in other areas. The pattern displayed by leaders in the present psychological theory group has more in common with founders of sociological specialties, suggesting that the greater commitment of leaders to their chosen specialties may typify the social sciences generally.

Perhaps the most interesting implication for the model itself to arise from the present study concerns its demonstrated usefulness in illuminating international differences in theory group evolution, since it rarely has been applied to groups having bases in different countries (Mullins, 1981, personal communication). As we have seen, apparent anomalies in the development of the theory within any given country often can be resolved by considering their relation to the broader, world-wide scene. For example, the recent production of major secondary works by the tiny Dutch group appears to depart from Mullins's model if only *intra*national developments are considered. In the broader context, however, the production of such materials makes sense in light of the availability of *inter*national social support (e.g., training and conferences) and intellectual resources (e.g., early texts and research) upon which the Dutch group could draw. For theory groups whose membership is not confined to a single country, consideration of international factors promoting or impeding their development obviously is necessary.

But does this imply that such multinational groups should be studied *only* as unified worldwide entities, without examining the differential social structural progress made by the individual countries they comprise? The answer depends on the intent of the investigator. In the present instance, PCT as a single theory group could be characterized simply as a specialty having its headquarters in Great Britain; networks in the U.S. and elsewhere could be seen simply as research outposts or extensions of the British system. While such a description might be quite adequate for some purposes, it would be wholly inadequate for others, such as predicting the degree of impact that the theory would have on its parent discipline in the United States.

In summary, the model for sociohistorical development of scientific disciplines propounded by Mullins seems to be quite useful in studying the emergence of theory groups in psychology, as well as in biology (Mullins, 1972) and sociology (Mullins, 1973). Such discrepancies as do occur between PCT's development and the model seem to represent unique social and intellectual variations in construct theory's evolution, rather than basic invalidations of the stage theory itself.

PROBLEMS AND PROSPECTS

At this point, I would like to reflect upon some of the unique issues that confront PCT at this stage in its development as a discipline. Like developmental crises in the lives of individuals, these issues represent important problems, the adequate resolution of which ultimately can strengthen the prospects for the theory group's healthy maturation. Because of their imminence, I have chosen to focus upon four such problems: the intellectual isolationism of the theory, its crisis of methodology, its relation to the new "cognitive" therapies, and the formation of an international organization for construct theorists. My treatment of each of these topics necessarily will be synoptic, since a full consideration of each would carry me too far from the focus of the present work. For this reason I often will have occasion to refer to the opinions of major figures within PCT without being able to afford the luxury of extensive quotation. Unless otherwise noted, such citations are based upon their personal communication to me in the context of the audiotaped interviews conducted from the summer of 1979 through the fall of 1980. [1]

A. The Intellectual Isolationism of PCT

By the term *intellectual isolationism* I mean the tendency of theory group members to disaffiliate themselves from other traditions of

thought and instead perpetuate a relatively *ingrown* pattern of communication with one another. This tendency has its origins in Kelly's dismissal of the formulations of his predecessors as if they were wholly
irrelevant to his own theory-building efforts. In the eyes of his most
sympathetic critics, this isolationism is noted simply as a curiosity. Reviewing Kelly's 1955 work, Bruner (1956, p. 356) remarks, "With respect to ancestry, Professor Kelly seems to care little for it. One misses
references to such works as Piaget's *The Child's Construction of Reality*,
the early work of Werner and the writings of Harry Stack Sullivan,
Lewin, and Allport—all of whom are on his side and are good allies to
boot." For reviewers working in those traditions (e.g., the psychoanalytic) from which Kelly borrows, but at the same time condemns,
Kelly's failure to provide reference to others becomes a reason to mini-
mize the import of his work. C. McArthur, also reviewing *The Psychology of Personal Constructs*, states, "The reader is left with a feeling of
irritation at finding billed as new discoveries things he can find almost
word for word in the earlier works of Freud or in the later works of those
who concerned themselves with the psychodynamics of normal personality" (1956, p. 307). At his worst moments, Kelly not only ignores but
also caricatures the image of persons offered by competing theorists (cf.,
Holland, 1970) in such a way that the genuine humanism and reason-
ableness of his own position stand out in even sharper contrast. Such
tactics lead his most caustic critics to infer that

> [Kelly] is exercised over a problem of his own making, for his broadsides
> are against a piece of psychoanalytic theory that was discarded in the
> 1920s. . . . It is incumbent upon a serious contributor to personality the-
> ory to know the dominant theory, especially if he criticizes it and erects
> his ostensibly new one on the basis of this criticism. Kelly writes as if he
> knows psychoanalysis, but he does not. (Appelbaum, 1969, p. 21)

S. A. Appelbaum then goes on to conclude—unfairly, I think—that
whatever popularity Kelly enjoyed could be attributed to clinical psychology's need for a "savior" during its early years of development.

> We are regularly offered a self-advertised avant-garde which all too often
> is merely reactionary and uninformed. Kelly apparently believed that he
> had to make up his own system, to start anew, to gather around him those
> who had the same complaints he had. He was a prophet with honor but

little prophesy, a spokesman more than a speaker, his eminence an accident of time. (Appelbaum, 1969, p. 25)

We need not agree with these conclusions in order to recognise the ease with which Kelly's manner of presentation leads members of other theory groups to dismiss the significance of his theory. Indeed, major figures *within* PCT (e.g., Salmon, Stringer) have also been critical of Kelly's failure to acknowledge his historical roots, in part because this leaves the theory more vulnerable to serious philosophical criticism (Adams-Webber).

Later construct theorists have been accused of perpetuating this isolationism, thereby weakening their position by ignoring work conducted by other camps. Thus L. Pervin (1973, p. 112), in his review of Bannister and Fransella's (1971) *Inquiring Man*, states, "The major limitation of the book is that the constructs used by the authors are at times . . . so tight and preemptive as to preclude incorporation of valuable insights from other theoretical points of view." Ryle, from his position on the periphery of the theory group, puts it more bluntly:

> [PCT's] main weakness is in its isolation, its self-isolation. Kelly's rather cavalier dismissal of everybody else, particularly psychoanalysis and behaviorism, seems to have been taken on board by most personal construct theorists, and a serious attempt to relate the theory to other attempts at dealing with human behavior has not taken place.

What these observers consistently (and rightly) point out is the extent to which PCT's insularity renders it less adequate as a comprehensive theory than it could be were it to take into account work arising from other traditions. What is missed in such accounts, however, is an appreciation of the important sociological function served by such isolationism, both at the theory's inception and in its later development. Holland touches upon the former when he explains

> The emergence of new personality theories is accompanied by ambivalence towards predecessors as the new theorists filter out what they need from the past and construct around it a new position. . . . For a new discipline to emerge it is necessary for strong expectation to be created that particular methods pursued in a certain theoretical direction will lead to new knowledge.

> In the continuous process of competition between intellectual for-
> mulations attached to various groups . . . groups sharing the same
> sphere of potential influence . . . will be at great pains to claim dis-
> tinctiveness for themselves. (1977, pp. 131–32, 163–64)

As Holland demonstrates, the textbook description of scientific progress
as a dispassionate and objective process of theorizing and experimentation fails to take into account the complex social processes actually involved in knowledge production. One such social factor is the need of
the theorist to attract adherents with sufficient commitment to the new
perspective to perform the laborious tasks of applying it, testing its implications, and so on. Thus, while Kelly's failure to credit his intellectual predecessors may have resulted partly from his limited exposure to
their work (see chap. 2), it also served to emphasize the distinctiveness,
and therefore the attractiveness, of his own formulations.

Nor is it surprising, from a sociology-of-science perspective, that
later construct theorists have helped perpetuate this isolationism. We
have already noted (chap. 7) that Bannister's publicly-advertised disdain
for "orthodox" British psychology helped attract to PCT the students
needed to pursue the group's research program. But a tendency toward
intellectual insularity is by no means a unique feature of PCT; it is a
quite regular occurrence in the course of disciplinary development. G.
Lemaine and his colleagues observe that as a field grows, "The propor-
tion of references to papers by authors not centrally engaged in the field
declines markedly" (G. Lemaine et al., 1976, p. 6). Similarly, Mullins
(1973) takes this inattention to work conducted outside the theory group
to be a defining characteristic of cluster-level activity. As such, it serves a
purpose, facilitating more cohesive communication ties and focusing
the developing group's efforts on a manageable set of theoretical
problems.

Yet, a recognition of the adaptiveness of isolationism *at early
stages of the group's development* does not imply that the theory should
not attempt to transcend such ingrown communication patterns as it
matures to specialty status. What is understandable (perhaps even necessary) for first-generation network members can be a serious failing
among second- or third-generation specialists. The challenge facing
PCT at the present historical moment is no longer that which confronted the theory group in 1955, or even in 1970. Rather, the present

challenge is that of revitalization through integration with other disciplines.

Fortunately, many present-day construct theorists recognize this requirement. One promising frontier for such integrative efforts (cited by Ryle and Adams-Webber, among others) is the modern cognitive work being done by experimental psychologists. W. H. Crockett articulates the need for construct theorists to explore this domain:

> People in construct theory feed on each other's work, and have not been influenced to the extent I think they should have by advances in cognitive psychology in particular. That, it seems to me, is changing, as people like Rosenberg move into the PCT framework, and as people who have been in PCT since it began, for example Mancuso, begin to adopt some of the tenets of current cognitive psychology.[2]

Construct theory could be enriched by taking into account work in other fields as well, particularly developmental psychology (Salmon, Mancuso), linguistics (Adams-Webber), social psychology (Duck), and even physiological psychology (Fransella). Moreover, the possibility of theoretical and metatheoretical cross-fertilization exists, with such diverse disciplines as the new philosophy of science (Mair), sociology, and (even) psychoanalysis (Holland). Holland summarizes PCT's current shift from a more isolationist to a more integrationist stance:

> I think there is new evidence, very fresh evidence at this point, that the theory is becoming so well established that it can begin to notice some of its limitations and some of the wider contexts that have to be linked into if the theory is to have a wider influence than just in psychotherapy or the very personal one-to-one situation.

B. The Crisis of Methodology

It is generally true of scientific activity that research areas tend to develop in response to major innovations, particularly technical innovations (Lemaine et al., 1976). Yet, as Holland points out, "There may be limitations on discovery imposed by the particular repertoire of techniques available to the investigator" (1977, p. 132). For this reason, critical attention should be aroused in cases when a specialty comes to rely heavily upon a single method or closely related set of methods, since such reliance tends to restrict both the type of questions the specialty addresses and the range of knowledge it ultimately produces.

From 1954 to 1981, members of the theory group associated with personal construct psychology produced 707 published *empirical* studies. Of these, 667—or *over 96 percent*—have employed some variant of repertory grid technique as their primary (or more often their only) means of operationalizing the variables being studied.[3] This degree of methodological constriction is remarkable and may be paralleled in the history of psychology only by Skinnerian behaviorism's reliance on the operant conditioning chamber and psychoanalysis's confidence in the "psychoanalytic method" as research paradigms that pre-empt all others. Given construct theory's singular devotion to grid technique, it is hardly surprising that the "major focus of research within the framework of PCT has been the formal analysis of conceptual structures and their evolution" (Adams-Webber, 1979, p. 42). (In practice, virtually all grid work focuses upon "the formal analysis of conceptual structures." Serious studies of their "evolution" are relatively rare.) For a theory that claims to be a "total psychology" (Fransella, 1978), this constriction in subject matter is appreciable.

Because of the several problems with grid technique—the restriction it places on research style and direction being only one—I believe that PCT presently is confronted with a *crisis of methodology*. Moreover, I believe it is one that is recognised (at some level of awareness) by many theory group members, though they differ, depending on their philosophical and empirical predilections, on the avenues they see leading toward its adequate resolution. I will try to sketch the situation as it is seen by the two major camps and then venture a prediction concerning the likely outcome of the present situation.

Before doing so, however, I should at least mention my own basic enthusiasm for grid technique. It seems to me to be a method that deserves a place in the armamentarium of personal construct theorists, and perhaps of psychologists more generally. Elsewhere (Neimeyer & Neimeyer, 1981a) I have summarized what I believe to be the major strengths of the method, though not all of them are used to full advantage in the existing literature. These include: 1) its applicability to longitudinal and developmental research; 2) its ability to tap multiple levels of construing, both verbal and nonverbal (cf. R. A. Neimeyer, 1981); 3) its usefulness in studying relationships between constructs (and between constructs and elements); 4) its considerable flexibility; 5) its elucidation of idiographic data in easily quantifiable form; and 6) its capacity to be adapted to the study of interpersonal, as well as individual, topics. A final advantage of grid technique, its articulation with PCT itself, will be considered later on.

But grids also have their problems, which can be classed roughly into two sets, the psychometric and the theoretical. Although the persons voicing these sets of criticisms do not cleanly divide into mutually exclusive categories, they do tend to fall into two identifiable clusters, the "grid methodologists" and the "PCT purists." Each cluster tends to perceive and emphasize a different set of concerns.

From the vantage point of the grid methodologists, the most significant problems with the technique concern its lack of psychometric soundness. Bavelas, Chan, and Guthrie (1976) exemplify this position. These authors conducted an extensive investigation of various "traits" (e.g., cognitive complexity, identification) derived from repertory grid matrices, both those generated by actual human subjects and those simulated by computer programs designed to produce matrices varying in their degree of "randomness." They concluded that little evidence existed for the reliability and (convergent) validity of any of the trait measures. These concerns are echoed by some who are closer to the PCT purist camp. Adams-Webber (1979, p. 213), for example, concludes his review of the empirical literature by noting that, "Considerable confusion has arisen because of a general disregard for basic issues of reliability and validity in developing operational definitions for specific constructs, such as differentiation, within PCT." A related issue has to do with the "external validity" of grids, i.e., the degree to which they are predictive of other behavior. As Adams-Webber (1979) points out, the evidence linking grid scores to specific observable behavior is quite sparse.

A number of other problems are posited at the psychometric level, for example, the potential restriction of the subject's response entailed by grids requiring dichotomous classification or rank-ordering of elements (Collett, 1979). A more general experimental criticism concerns the common failure to assess the "reactivity" involved in grid studies. Thus, Collett remarks:

> The investigator may choose whether to accept the completed matrix as a summary of the subjects' actual opinions or as some convenient expression of what the subject assumes to be required in that situation. The

delicate task of deciding between these conceptions is seldom aired by
those who work with the grid. . . . There is absolutely no justification for
assuming that the grid method is somehow immune to these reactive
processes. (1979, p. 248)

A. T. Ravenette (1977) concedes this point when he suggests that the
constructs a subject records on the grid are not *elicited* from some pre-
existing repertoire, but are *created* in response to experimental demands.

The solution to these problems, from the grid methodologist perspective, is most likely to come from increased attention to the principles of sound experimental design (Bonarius) and further refinement in
grid technique itself (Collett, 1979). P. Rathod is one of the most visible
representatives of this point of view. In a recent report, for example, he
argues that "An idiographic instrument is reliable to the extent that the
interpretations based on it remain invariant over differences in sampling
information" (1980, p. 333). He then examines the reliability of principal components solutions of grids of various sizes, concluding that
they are "considerably invariant over the sampling of additional grid
data." Elsewhere, Rathod (1981) critically evaluates several methods for
analyzing grids that vary in their level of mathematical and technical
sophistication and makes the case that construct theorists could upgrade
their methodology by incorporating the insights of statisticians and numerical taxonomists who work with similar data matrices.

From the vantage point of PCT purists, the problems with current
grid work are more basic than can be solved by further methodological
refinements, or even by the development of more rigorous experimental
designs that control for reactivity, demonstrate the relation of test scores
to behavior, and so on. As it is usually articulated, the basic problem is
that psychologists have become so fascinated with grid-induced rid-
dles— "griddles," to use Brian Little's (1979) apt phrase—that they fail
to ground their increasingly esoteric methods in a suitable comprehensive theory, preferably PCT. Thus Adams-Webber traces the confusion
that surrounds many grid measures to the fact that "investigators and
clinicians have employed forms of grid test in research and assessment
which have no logical relation to the principles of PCT" (1979, p. 20).
Similarly, Landfield cautions, "It should be kept in mind that the use of
a construct technique does not necessarily mean that it is being used in
the best spirit of the theory" (1980, p. 67). In opposition to figures like

Collett (1979), Slater, Ryle, and Rathod, who hold that grids can be used meaningfully independently of PCT, purists contend that such use not only vitiates grid technique itself but detracts from the theory-building efforts that are, or should be, the construct theorist's major task (Duck, Landfield, Bannister, Fransella). It follows from this that methodological ambiguities can only be resolved by tethering technique more closely to theory.

A second, and perhaps even more basic criticism corresponds to the sociological observation with which this section opened: that the characteristics embodied in a theory group's technical resources subtly shape the sort of questions it asks. The elemental, verbalized antonyms invoked by the subject to compare and contrast elements on a standard repertory grid undoubtedly conduce to an interpretation of construing as a highly cognitive affair. Thus, Mair rhetorically asks, "How much of PCT research has focused explicitly on constructs as conceptual templets rather than as guides to action?" (1977a, p. 141). Bannister gets to the heart of the problem:

> One of the things that jammed the theory down a bit was that, despite all the developments in the grid—which are in some ways admittedly impressive—we've still been using, as it were, rather static, cross-section methods. We've found ways of cutting in, putting the slide under microscope. . . . But we haven't found ways of following process, seeing flow, and making sense out of it, which is very dangerous when you're dealing with something that is essentially *about* flow, essentially about people living over time.

The most fundamental criticism from the purist perspective, then, is that *grids reify precisely those aspects of PCT that are least adequate*. By their very nature, they tend to obscure a conceptualization of construing as an essentially *temporal* rather than *spatial* affair (c.f. Radley, 1977). But responsibility for this emphasis does not reside solely with technique; some responsibility must be shared by the theory which engendered it. As Mair observes:

> The presentation of PCT, I think, leads into ways of thinking that are very tight, rather than looser. "Structured," "bounded," I mean the whole adjective issue. . . . Adjectives have become almost gold as far as construct theory is concerned. But *verbs* don't get much of a look (laughs)! I mean it's a theory which, I think, is a theory of action, or process, and the

rest, and which doesn't get many verbs. . . . And why is that? It's because somehow in writing the theory—the particular example of the grid
can be used—some kind of "cloppity-clop" notion, a cybernetic, information, trait-related notion, is still very much around. . . .

A lot of people say this is a radical alternative psychology, and so
on. Mostly, I don't think it is that at all. I feel there are fingers stretched
out, in Kelly, towards what *is* a radically different psychology, if you are to
come to terms with a much elaborated and deeper sense of "knowing."

From this second, metatheoretical variant of the purist position,
the crisis of methodology is resolvable neither by greater technical and
experimental sophistication (the grid methodologists' solution) nor by
simply trying method more firmly to theory (as advocated by most PCT
purists). Neither solution is adequate, since *both method and theory
embody the same flaws.* Kelly can be credited with having glimpsed the
outlines of what psychology might one day become, and, at his best
moments, he even anticipated some of its contours (as in his treatment
of loosening, threat, anxiety, and so forth). But his writings, particularly
his earlier ones, only begin to articulate the directions in which such an
inquiry might lead. As such, they cannot be considered the criterion
against which grid technique (or any other method) can be measured.
In this light, the only adequate resolution of the present crisis will
evolve slowly, from basic theoretical, metatheoretical, and philosophical refinements. Ironically, it may hinge on the ultimate obsolescence
of PCT as it now exists.

At the outset of this section I promised to venture a prediction as
to the outcome of the methodological crisis that now confronts the theory group. Unfortunately, I am not optimistic about the prospects for a
healthy resolution. I believe the rift between the methodologists and the
purists to be too deep and wide to be bridged, even at present, and
indications are that it will continue to grow as the former become more
mathematically sophisticated and the latter turn increasingly to (new)
theoretical pursuits. Such diversification of group members typically
accelerates when a group reaches specialty status. But in the case of
PCT, the prospects of achieving a resolution that most group members
could endorse is made still less likely by (1) the unevenness of social-
structural progress displayed by PCT communities in various countries,
and (2) the (relatively) elite status accorded grid methodologists, at least
in the U.K. The first factor will serve to frustrate a widely agreed-upon
solution because the relative fragmentation of the theory group outside

Great Britain will slow the dissemination of whatever methodological skills might eventually supplant or extend existing techniques. Even the widespread availability of intellectual materials concerning the new methods cannot be expected to counteract this effect since the mastery of new technical resources seems to be transmitted mainly through direct apprenticeship. This is supported by the fact that existing state-of-the-art grid analysis methods, as represented by Slater's (1965, 1976) programs, have found only very limited use outside the U.K., and then principally by persons who have studied directly with him.

The second factor, that elite status tends to attach to sophistication in grid technique, further hampers movement toward crisis resolution. This is so because it is clear that a great many significant contributors are sympathetic to purist criticisms of the method and hence are unlikely to rally around any solution that consists simply of a psychometric refinement of existing techniques. At the same time, the fact that grid users can claim at least a modicum of respectability within the (quantitatively oriented) parent discipline means that powerful social and professional inducements would have to be sacrificed in order for such techniques to be abandoned. Short of a complete "paradigm shift" in psychology as a whole, this seems unlikely to happen.

For these and other reasons, I believe a "methodological revolution" that would (re)unite PCT as a theory group to be a remote possibility. It seems far more probable that intragroup divisiveness will become increasingly apparent in the future, until the theory group as a specialty becomes so differentiated that it loses its distinctiveness and gradually blends into the "normal science" scene once again. If this is the case, then methodological advances will be of local, rather than specialty-wide, interest. Of course, this does not mean that their intellectual significance is reduced. In fact, some such advances presently are taking place and are beginning to attract the attention they deserve (e.g., Thomas's and Space's development of interactive computer administration of grids, Duck's and Viney's exploration of nongrid methods). The number of such innovations has grown, rather than declined, in recent years.

Finally, I will close with one more remark about the future, putting forward a hope rather than a prediction. If grid technique ultimately proves to be interesting but too restrictive (and I believe it will), and if there are at least some seeds in Kelly's writing that deserve to be cultivated (and I believe there are), then I hope that a few construct theorists will begin to explore seriously the radically different methodologies that may enable them to do so. This exploration may well lead beyond the frontiers of psychology altogether and into fields as diverse as linguistics, ethnomethodology, symbolic interactionism, and cognitive anthropology. The obstacles to crossing such disciplinary boundaries are very great (Holland, 1977), but the dangers of methodological provincialism are far greater.[4]

C. Relationship to the Cognitive Therapies

Perhaps one of the most sweeping and widely publicized developments in the field of clinical psychology to take place in the last decade has been the emergence of the various "cognitive therapies" (Kendall and Hollon, 1979). Historically, these therapeutic approaches represent a convergence of two major streams of influence, cognitive psychology and behavior modification. Starting in the late 1960s, behaviorists like J. R. Cautela (1967) and L. P. Ullman (1970) began applying the principles of functional analysis to the study and modification of cognitive processes, construed as "covert behaviors." At about the same time, therapists like A. Ellis (1969) and A. T. Beck (1970) began to explore the relationship between their avowedly rational, or cognitive, approaches and traditional behavior therapy. As M. Mahoney and D. Arnkoff (1978, p. 689) note, the general response to this merger "has been one of enthusiasm and fervid research," yielding works of major importance by Beck, J. Rush, B. Shaw and G. Emery (1979), M. Goldfried and M. Merbaum (1973), A. Bandura (1977), M. Mahoney (1974), D. Meichenbaum (1974), and many others.

When leading representatives of this cognitive behavioral movement reflect upon their intellectual heritage, they frequently credit Kelly's personal construct theory as having contributed importantly to their own integrative work. Beck et al. (1979), for example, acknowledge Kelly's influence on the development of their own cognitive therapy of depression, and Mahoney and Arnkoff (1978, p. 691), more generally, regard Kelly as an "early cognitive-learning cultivator" who may have been one of "the founding fathers of our current trend." The fact that cognitive-behavioral editors (e.g., Kendall, 1984; Mahoney, 1980; Merluzzi, Glass, & Genest, 1981) recently have solicited contributed book chapters from construct theorists further testifies to the congruence that cognitively oriented therapists see between their own work and that being conducted within the framework in PCT.

My aim in this section will be to address the relationship that exists between construct theory and the cognitive therapies. In keeping with the social emphasis of this work, I will concentrate on describing the reactions of members of the PCT theory group to these approaches, since this will suggest the extent to which an active collaboration between the two groups is possible.

A few theory group members perceive a basic "compatibility" between Kellyan theorizing and cognitive therapeutic formulations. G. Neimeyer takes this position, and sees it deriving from their common intellectual ancestry:

> When I think of cognitive therapies, I think of Ellis's Rational Emotive Therapy, maybe some of Meichenbaum's work, Goldfried's rational restructuring, and Beck's work on depression. . . . And I think that they have a great deal in common with Kelly's construct theory. Most importantly, I think they probably draw from similar sorts of original sources (e.g., Korzybski's general semantics), and I think that these common sources of origin have not been sufficiently credited either by the cognitive approaches or by Kelly himself.

Bieri is in basic agreement with this point of view, observing that "there's no question that a lot of recent cognitive approaches in personality and psychotherapy reflect . . . some of the same concerns that [Kelly] had earlier elaborated."

But this clearly is a minority position. G. Neimeyer is one of the few theory group members who sees "a possibility for an exciting interface" between PCT and cognitive therapy, and even he cautions that Kelly's fundamental conception of construing as a more-than-just-cognitive activity may become adulterated in the process.

A number of other figures (e.g., Landfield, McCoy) acknowledge a limited degree of correspondence between the two approaches but believe that the recent cognitive work has little to contribute to the more theoretically sophisticated PCT perspective. Cromwell articulates this sentiment:

> Obviously there are some commonalities here, but I believe anyone who has been thoroughly trained in a Kelly personal construct point of view

winds up being a little bit disappointed in the approach of a lot of the cognitive therapies and cognitive personality theorists. . . . In dealing with the notions of affect, emotions, and feelings, it appears to me even now that Kelly was decades ahead of his time and the current cognitive theorists have not really caught up.

From this vantage point, personal construct *theory* is unlikely to be extended in any important way through its affiliation with cognitive therapy, although it may profit by gaining a wider audience (Dingemans, Landfield, Crockett). The clearly pragmatic basis for such an affiliation is suggested in a statement by Epting:

> My own interests lie in the direction of elaborating PCT in the direction of phenomenological and existential positions within psychology, just because I believe they're bigger ideas than the ones being pursued in cognitive psychology. Although the way to reach the rest of psychology is certainly through identifying with cognitive psychology, so that I can't argue with anybody who wants to take construct theory in that direction. But in truth, I don't really think that it has much to do with it, although Kelly wrote it initially so badly in some respects that it sounded like a cognitive theory. I think that was a mistake on Kelly's part, one that he later admitted, but one that he didn't have time to correct before his death.

Most PCT purists see Kelly's (sometimes inadequate) attempts to transcend the cognition-emotion-behavior trichotomy as the very essence of his theory and, hence, experience some discomfort at being identified with an explicitly cognitive movement. Holland summarizes the current situation: "Cognitive psychologists are finding links [to PCT] to the embarrassment of personal construct theorists."

While these theory group members generally are willing to acknowledge *some* commonality between PCT and cognitive approaches (if only to "piggyback" their work to larger audiences), others are unable to concede even this degree of similarity between the two. Stringer, for instance, states flatly that he sees "no relation here," and Mair adds, "I'm not aware of much in terms of cognitive behavior therapy that says anything to me at all." The rejection of these new therapies by many in the PCT community is prompted not so much by technical differences between the two groups (e.g., in their psychotherapeutic procedures) but by their basic theoretical and metatheoretical incompatibilities. Salmon, for example, takes issue with the cognitivists' philosophical realism. "I think behaviorism *a priori* defines reality independent of the perspective of the individual. And since cognition ought at least to be in some sense phenomenological, I see [cognitive behaviorism] as a doomed approach. If Kelly's approach is brought into this mishmash I should see no hope for any of it." Leitner voices similar misgivings:

> I see very serious dangers in identifying ourselves too closely with these very recent cognitive approaches to personality and psychotherapy. . . . These "cognitive" positions are essentially behavioristic positions in sheep's clothing. I personally find many of these positions being in a sense very antithetical to construct theory when you look at the image of man implicit in them.

Fransella extends this criticism and contends that the cognitive therapies incorporate Kellyan insights, albeit in diluted form:

> They're subsumed by construct theory, aren't they? I mean, they're poor man's construct theories, basically. Aren't they? What do they do, except look at people in terms of how they construe things? . . . But they're behavior therapies, cognitive behavior therapies. Nowhere in those cognitive behavior therapist's "learning theory" is there anything that accounts for what they're doing. So they're cheating.
> At a recent "Models of Man" conference, the Skinnerians there refused to say ultimately what their model of man was. They couldn't, because they couldn't keep doing what they're doing if they had to say, "Well, it's man-the-automaton." Because they know they're not automata. And until they come to grips with what they're talking about, I don't think they're going to get anywhere. I mean, if they want to cheat, fine, but I don't want anything to do with them.

Mancuso puts the rejection of the cognitive movement in its strongest form:

> These people who call themselves cognitive psychotherapists are full of hogwash. There is nothing cognitive about their work. They're very mechanistic. All they're saying is that if you talk to yourself and give yourself goodies, you're going to become a different person. I don't think they have a handle on it at all.

For the purposes of the present work it is unnecessary to assess the validity of any of these claims or counterclaims.[5] What is important is to realize that most leaders within PCT are at best lukewarm concerning the prospects for meaningful collaboration with cognitive-behavior theorists, and at worst are openly antagonistic to such collaboration. Rejection of the cognitive work, when it occurs, is based on a critical evaluation, not of its clinical methods, but of its metatheoretical implications.[6] Construct theorists fear that the incorporation of their formulations into a cognitive-behavioral framework will result in a distortion of those tenets of PCT that are closest to the heart of Kellyan theory: an image of persons as active, interpretive agents, the impassioned nature of construing, and so forth. Indeed, it seems *probable* that such unique features of the theory will be missed by those who approach it from a more behavioral background. Consider the following remarks by D. C. Rimm and J. C. Masters:

> Kelly's (1955) fixed-role therapy bears a remarkable similarity to Rational Emotive Therapy in terms of its philosophical basis as well as its here-and-now action orientation. Nonetheless, Kelly's manner of presentation, while logically appealing, is quite esoteric, and this may in part account for why his impact on practitioners has not been nearly so great as that of Ellis. (1979, pp. 379–380)

These authors seem oblivious to the fundamental philosophical differences between the two therapies (e.g., in their degree of prescriptiveness cf. R. Neimeyer, 1984b), differences that are apparent even to construct theorists who are quite interested in an RET approach (Rowe). Moreover, they imply that if Kelly's theory were less "esoteric," that is, if it were couched in more common language, it would have greater impact. It is just this tendency to "underdimension" PCT (e.g., by interpreting Kelly's "construct" as "cognitive") that leads PCT purists to shy away from close collaboration with the cognitive-behavioral movement.

But this is not a unique failing of cognitive-behaviorists. It is generally appreciated by sociologists of science that *knowledge decays in the process of standardization.* As Mulkay explains:

> Meaning is lost by translation in science as well as in literature. Points of obscurity and conceptual difficulties are overlooked. The limitations of underlying assumptions are forgotten. And the balance and emphasis of

the original formulation are altered to meet the needs of new areas of application. In addition, because the knowledge, technical skills and standards of adequacy of the various audiences involved are likely to be quite diverse, the standardized version must be considerably simplified. (1979, pp. 58–59)

Therefore a certain loss of subtlety and meaning must be expected if construct theoretical formulations are to have a broad impact within the parent discipline. As a review of the foregoing remarks by major figures within PCT will disclose, there are broad national as well as individual differences within the theory group as to how much compromise of meaning should be allowed in order to assure the theory a wider audience. Specifically, proportionately more *Americans* seem willing to tolerate some loss of content, at least initially, in order to publish PCT work in cognitively oriented journals and potentially attract fresh interest in the theory. Major *British* figures, in contrast, are almost uniform in their rejection of such a position, largely because they fear the metatheoretical compromise that such a rapprochement might entail. In light of the differential degree of social-structural progress made by the theory group in the two nations, this divergence in opinion is not surprising. Construct theorists in the U.S. are hampered, both by the lower degree of institutionalization of their work and by their more "revolutionary" reputation, from having widespread impact on American psychology as a whole. For them, partial identification with a clearly "elite" group (like the cognitive-behavior therapists) at least assures them that their view will be heard, and perhaps even help shape the future of their parent discipline. Such a prospect is not fantastic, given the right social conditions. As Mullins (1973, p. 129) observes, a "small, coherent group can produce massive changes in the theoretical orientation of a field."

In the U.K., on the other hand, the situation is very different. British theory group members have made considerable progress towards institutionalizing their position (on editorial boards, in the BPS, etc.) and can claim a measure of elite status for their methodological prowess. Even the more unorthodox theoretical implications of PCT occasionally are aired in the classroom and conference hall. For British construct theorists, then, there is nothing to gain and much precious distinctiveness to loose by affiliating too closely with the cognitive-behavioral tradition.

For this reason, the adequate resolution of PCT's problematic relation to the cognitive therapies necessarily will entail different courses of action for construct theorists in different countries. In particular, for Americans to refuse to carry on a dialogue with (receptive) cognitive therapists would be to perpetuate their "intellectual isolationism" (see sect. A) and preclude their participation in the "cognitive revolution" that is changing the emphasis of mainstream psychology in the U.S. Collaboration with the new approaches need not require American construct theorists to capitulate to a mechanistic paradigm, but it may require them patiently to emphasize and re-emphasize the meta-theoretical commitments that inform their work. In the U.K., on the other hand, this laborious but potentially fruitful task is less urgent, not only because PCT is more institutionalized in Britain, but because the cognitive therapies are less so. If the theory group is unable to tolerate different strategies for development in different nations, then its impact may be limited to those geographical regions where it is already best established.

D. Formation of an International Organization

From a sociological point of view, resolution of this final problem is perhaps the most critical. It concerns the extent to which PCT, as a theory group, should seek to institutionalize its activity through the formation of its own professional organization. Of course, steps toward institutionalization already have been taken, especially in the U.K., where PCT to some extent has penetrated existing societies and journals. But the present issue raises difficult, divisive questions not entailed in earlier British efforts, in large part because it lifts to a conscious level social organizational processes that ordinarily take place outside focal awareness. Thus, the decision to organize in a more formal way puts the question in crystalline form: Should the theory group consciously seek to promote its own development?

The fact that these organizational issues did not emerge for PCT until it had passed from cluster to specialty status in the mid-1970s provides a kind of support for Mullins's (1973) model, since it would predict that heightened concerns about institutionalizing the theory group's work would coincide with the advent of looser social-structural ties among its members. The specific instigating context for this discussion was the Nebraska Symposium of 1975, later dubbed The First International Congress in Personal Construct Psychology (see chap. 6). The success of the congress prompted several practical questions: Would there be a second congress? When? Who would organize it? Where would it be held? Would it follow or diverge from the style set by the Nebraska example? Fransella, after some discussion with other prominent members of the PCT community (e.g., Bannister, Mair), announced that a second congress would be held two years hence in England. This announcement was received with general enthusiasm by construct theorists in England and abroad.

With the success of the second congress in 1977, it became clear that further conferences would be held at regular intervals and that some mechanism for deciding where such "officially sanctioned" meetings would convene would be required. Again, an "informal" get-together of natural leaders (the group grew somewhat to include figures like Salmon, Epting, Bonarius, and Landfield) decided the issue, and the same mechanism served to establish the location of future congresses through 1983.

Gradually, however, the decision-making process has become more politicized. Beginning with the 1979 congress, held in Oxford, England, announcements concerning subsequent congresses have been made in a final plenary session. The assent of conference attenders to the meeting location suggested by the informal "leaders" of the group was signaled by simple voice vote, or later, by hand count. This mechanism was expedient and unproblematic as long as (a) planning was short-range, e.g., two years hence, and (b) only one group put forward a proposed congress site and date. But in recent years neither of these conditions has been met. At the 1981 Canadian Congress, for example, there was general agreement that the 1983 congress would be held in Boston and that Landfield, Epting, G. Neimeyer, and others would share responsibility for working out its format, making arrangements for accommodations, and so forth. But the proposal that the 1985 congress be sponsored by the highly visible Bannister-Fransella cluster in England was opposed vigorously by an Australian lobby led by Phil Candy. The "revolt" ultimately foundered on practical grounds, when the majority of attenders present (particularly those aligned with the large British and American networks) voted it down on the rationale that the extraordinary expense entailed by travel to Australia would preclude the attendance of many theory group members.

This conflict was sharpened still further in the plenary session of the 1983 Boston congress, when several viable proposals emerged for the location of the 1987 meeting. Alan Brown began by volunteering to convene the meeting in Alberta, Canada, a plan that was opposed in part because of the geographic remoteness of the location. A second suggestion by Jeff Katz to hold the congress in New York City was resisted because of its proximity to the recent Boston site. Although Candy was absent, a renewed proposal for an Australian congress was spearheaded by Linda Viney, but again was opposed on grounds of travel costs. Bill Perry then offered to sponsor the meeting in Honolulu, arguing that not only would it be a conducive setting, but also that it would be closer than other alternatives to the Australasian network. The proposal inspired passionate debate, with McCoy, Terence Keen, and both Neimeyers supporting the Hawaiian congress site, and several prominent American and British attenders (including Bannister) opposing it on the argument that flight costs—like those to Australia—would dramatically cut European participation. An alternative site in the Netherlands was offered by Bonarius, Jan van Rooij, and Roelf Takens and was quickly adopted by the majority by a show of hands. The vote was overridden, however, when proponents of the Perry proposal militated for conformity to Roberts Rules of Order and brought to the floor a similar vote for all locations. A hand count revealed a preference for the Hawaiian congress, and the earlier decision was reversed.

The evident need of the theory group to decide the course of its own social and professional development and to settle competing interests (as in the case of two or more groups who want to sponsor an upcoming congress) suggests the importance of asking the questions, What level of social-organizational development is appropriate for the theory group at this point in its sociohistorical development? Is it time to consider formalizing an organization of personal construct psychologists?

I put this latter question to over two dozen major contributors in PCT in the course of personal or taped interviews with them and discovered that the theory group was sharply divided on the advisability of such a move. Those opposing formal organization (Mancuso, Ravenette, Ryle, Duck, Salmon, Rosenberg, Mair, Radley, Adams-Webber, and Dingemans) frequently acknowledge that organizing could facilitate communication among group members but fear that this communication would be too "ingrown," ultimately reinforcing PCT's tendency toward insularity from the parent discipline. Duck emphasizes a related problem:

> As soon as you set up a separate organization, you're asserting a separate identity and so on and not being incorporated in things that people are doing. And it seems to me that one of the main problems with being a PCT person at this moment is that outsiders regard us as a separate group of people who are not to be dealt with necessarily.

Several of the remarks by this group also reflect a general suspicion regarding the effects of institutionalization itself. Adams-Webber, for example, contends that "organizations may promote the status of a theory's adherents, but they do not foster the intellectual integrity of the people involved." Furthermore, he stresses that "theories should be evaluated on the basis of their logical validity and their usefulness in organizing empirical facts," and suspects that formalizing social support for a position may detract from that process. Ravenette's remark exemplifies this more general concern: "Institutions kill, and if they don't kill, they change the emphasis to the preservation of the institution rather than the development of that for which the institution was formed. This is a very general statement, but I believe it to be true." This sentiment finds its strongest expression in a statement by Mancuso:

> I'm totally opposed to formalizing organizations that are built around trying to pursue a particular line in psychology. . . . I think that if we can't make a dent on the field as a whole we have no business in the field. I enjoy our little get-togethers with people who are like-minded, the kind of thing we've been having in congresses and so on, and those are fine. . . . But the minute this organization will become formal, the minute they talk about electing a president, that's when I quit.

A second sizable group (including Bieri, Crockett, Epting, Cromwell, Fransella, Holland, Rowe, G. Neimeyer, Leitner, and Rathod) is generally supportive of constituting an organization with somewhat firmer structure and procedures than exist at present. Like those who oppose further institutionalization, this second group also takes into account the pros and cons of doing so but concludes, on balance, that the former outweigh the latter. Epting is representative of this position:

I can only see advantages. No, I can see some disadvantages if we were to solidify into a tight little group that would be very defensive and turn people off. . . . [But] an effective institution could develop that could promote the elaboration of construct theory, and I really think we can't avoid formalizing it. . . . If I had to come down to a binary choice between whether to formalize it or whether not to, I would go on the side of coming up with some kind of organization.

A number of the theory group members who take this stand point out that it does not represent a sharp departure from tradition but merely extends social processes that have been operative for some time. G. Neimeyer states:

The reason that I would stand behind, or back, formalizing an international organization is that basically I would see that as doing little more than making explicit what's already happening on an implicit level. . . . There's a natural course of formalization going on, and I think that turning our attention to it and making that explicit may enable us to make some decisions consciously that otherwise we might just take for granted or make unconsciously.

He acknowledges one major drawback to this course of action—that further formalization could foster intellectual inbreeding—and then continues:

A second major disadvantage I would see is making explicit political struggles [within the theory group] that . . . are probably not as prominent under present conditions. . . . Thirdly, at the point that the theory becomes formalized there is going to be more and more of a critical reaction against construct theory.

Of course, this third disadvantage also has its positive aspects, as he points out: "The better target you give for someone to take aim at, the better criticism you're likely to get."

Those who advocate organization often point out that present arrangements, though adequate initially, are rapidly becoming outmoded as the theory group continues to increase in size. Thus Fransella, a member of the "natural leadership" since the beginning, remarked at the 1979 conference, "I feel very strongly that we need to come to some decision at this conference as to what is going to happen with an organization, because our group is just too big to go on with this." Holland adds sociological weight to this conclusion when he notes that "it is a common problem for networks and social movements, that they reach a crisis point where they are so big that it is difficult to go on in an informal, haphazard, fashion. So I think that [PCT] is now beginning to organize."

If these observations are valid, that PCT has outgrown its existing informal structure or soon will do so, then the only option does not appear to be the overly bureaucratized, self-perpetuating, intellectually stifling organization dreaded by so many theory group members. As Landfield points out:

> My own view is that what we need to do is to state our purposes. What is it that those of us in personal construct theory want to happen, and then do we feel that some kind of organization . . . with a little bit greater formality . . . will enhance the possibility of our doing whatever it is we want to do? . . . For example, we might have a system where people would be nominated from different areas of the world. Perhaps there would be a committee of five people who would decide on their own chairman, and then that committee would simply be responsible for finding someone to take over the responsibility of the congress every two years. They might eventually . . . have some jurisdiction over the Clearing House.

The principle being evoked here is one of *minimum sufficient organization* to achieve desired ends, a position advocated by the sociologist H. A. Becker at the congress held in Holland in 1979. Framing the issue in this way permits us to explore the kinds of institutional structure that might support our intentions as a theory group. As Bannister emphasizes, there is ample room to create unconventional organizational alternatives compatible with the pluralistic philosophy of PCT itself.

> So I think we need to start, not with the question "Can we organize in the traditional sense?," but if you want to get people interested in construct theory, how would we go about it—from a construct theory point of view? I'm not sure what the answer would be, but I'm sure it would be one that other people would see as looser, and more changing.

He goes on to voice his fundamental antagonism to traditional, hierarchical organizations:

I am prepared to keep contending, that is, actively opposing and fighting against the tendency to simply replace me and my mob, if you like, by somebody else and some other mob. And I don't, in a sense, care whether they're better or worse qualified. The battle becomes about the way we are going to do things, not about who's doing them.

If reactions like Bannister's provide impetus for construct theorists to evolve a kind of organization that is less hierarchical and less restrictive than conventional alternatives, but that is nonetheless *sufficient to the group's needs*, then they will serve a useful end. But if they serve mainly to impede formalization, on the grounds that *any* institutionalization is inherently dehumanizing, then they may do more to stunt the development of PCT than promote it. It is worth realizing, with Mullins (1973), that specialty-level development in a field necessarily entails the creation of a more bureaucratized communication structure than was characteristic of the earlier cluster stage, if only because the group has grown too large to conduct its affairs with the face-to-face informality that was possible when it had only a few members.

The Critical Upshot

I have presented four problems currently besetting construct theory: its intellectual isolationism, its crisis of methodology, its relation to the cognitive therapies, and its movement toward professional organization. By examining these issues against the backdrop of the theory group's sociohistorical development, I have tried to demonstrate that each of these problems has a social dimension. Just as an individual's early spontaneous, egocentric development gradually yields to a more planful self-elaboration encompassing a keener awareness of the social context, so, too, the maturing theory group eventually may predicate its further development on a reflexive understanding of its sociological status. Perhaps personal construct theory has attained this level of disciplinary maturity.

A field takes on pertinence under a definite complex of social and intellectual conditions. For construct theory, these conditions included behaviorism's hegemony on the psychological scene, a condition that prevailed throughout the 1960s. In such a context, the rigorous personalism of Kelly's theory and its associated grid technique offered an alternative, both to the arid objectivism of behavioral formulations and to the abstruse subjectivism of "third force" psychologies. Introduced into a theoretical climate inimical to its survival, construct theory's self-reliant isolationism was both defensive and defensible.

But as Kelly (1955) has reminded us, the universe changes along a dimension of time. This is no less true of the universe of intellectual discourse. Certainly psychology as a discipline has changed since the 1950s and has assimilated, consciously or unconsciously, many "construct theoretical" concepts in the process. If construct theory is to retain its vitality, it must be willing to move beyond its older Kellyan knowledge claims and participate more fully in these broader developments. As I noted earlier, there are signs that this reintegration is beginning to occur.

If this revitalization is to be sustained, however, social developments in the theory group must keep pace with the intellectual. This requirement follows from the reflexive nature of social science: we draft our theories in part as theories of our own lives. Thus, by perpetuating the small and intimate communication system characteristic of "the good old days of clusterhood," construct theorists organizationally reinforce the personalistic emphasis of the theory to which they subscribe. Were they seriously to elaborate their social-communicative network along more complex bureaucratic lines, they might more quickly confront the limitations of PCT as a theory of social life.

In the usual case, social science, as a body of knowledge, must adjust itself to fit the social reality it seeks to describe. Occasionally, however, a social scientific theory group must reverse this process by adjusting its internal social reality (i.e., its communication processes and its organizational framework) to match its own knowledge output. Personal construct theory has not really matched the complexity and diversity of its own published literature, which meshes with numerous specialties in the social sciences, with a comparably complex social communication structure that would link it more firmly with other theory groups. However difficult these social adjustments may be, I believe they can, and must, take place.

NOTES

Chapter 1

1. As this statement of purpose implies, I will not endeavor here to review the intellectual "content" of personal construct psychology, except in the most general way. Definitive accounts of the theoretical, clinical, and research issues historically given attention by construct workers are provided by Bonarius (1965), Adams-Webber (1979), and R. A. Neimeyer (1984b).

2. Although general theoretical consistency is reinforced during the cluster stage, infighting on minor issues is important within the group and is to be expected (Mullins, 1973, p. 90). In Lakatos's (1978) terms, this represents agreement on the "hard core" of shared theoretical commitments, but disagreement on the "protective belt" of dispensible hypotheses. Although delineation of these features of PCT will not be attempted in any rigorous way in the present work, such delineation would be theoretically valuable, particularly in light of the emergence of related paradigms (e.g., some of the newer "cognitive therapies") that appear to share some of PCT's empirical propositions while differing subtley in their core commitments. Some of these themes will be addressed in Chapter 8.

Chapter 2

1. Ray Holland (1977) has provided just this kind of psychosocial analysis of several important self-theorists. Although Kelly is not among the group of theorists whose lives he examines in detail, his observations concerning the style of argument Kelly uses to discredit his "opposition" (especially behaviorism,

sociology, and psychoanalysis) clearly bear upon the personal, professional, and societal contexts within which Kelly was working. See Holland (1970, 1977, 1981).

2. The sense of humanity's "noble quest," or "honorable struggle," that pervades PCT finds expression even in Kelly's earliest writings. For example, a portion of the text of his first publication, his award-winning oration in the Peace Oratorial Contest held at Friends University during his sophomore year, reads:

> Why have war? The psychologist says that war is inevitable, that man is destined to struggle, and that to refuse to fight is cowardly. To refuse to struggle is cowardly, but there is more honorable struggle than that which hurls both our neighbor and ourselves toward the dark oblivion from which even modern genius of civilization cannot rescue. A true manhood finds realms to conquer other than his neighbor's territory. (Kelly, 1924, p. 79)

3. The parallel between Kelly's work and that of the European phenomenologists is so striking that it once—mistakenly—led me to assume that he was well acquainted with their work (R. A. Neimeyer, 1977).

Incidentally, Kelly's tendency to reinvent a generally more *optimistic* "existential" psychology, one that clearly articulated the human capacity for progress and "elaboration" of one's identity, seems to reflect his life as well. Certainly for Kelly, who rose above a relatively constraining rural fundamentalist background to become an internationally known psychologist, the pronouncement that "no one need to be a prisoner of his biography" (Kelly, 1955) must have carried deep personal significance.

4. For a detailed account of environmental influences on Kelly's thought during the Fort Hays years, see Zelhart and Jackson (1983).

Chapter 3

1. Authors are considered to espouse similar formulations if they (1) cite similar sources; (2) are known to be colleagues or students of one another, or all of a third person; and (3) are considered similar by themselves and others (Mullins, 1973, p. 12).

2. A similar strategy for identifying group members has been employed by Crane (1972) in her study of "invisible colleges" in science. However, she chose the more liberal criterion of authorship or coauthorship of a single relevant paper to identify contributors to a research tradition. A detailed account of the construction of the current bibliography may be obtained from the author.

3. Professional biographies for American, British, and other contributors (including area, year, and university in which graduate degree was completed, and institutional affiliations from 1954 to 1981) may be obtained from the author. These data were omitted from the text because of space considerations.

4. The fact that only a small percentage of the nearly one hundred "Thursday-Nighters" eventually published significantly in PCT accords with Mullins's observation that active adherents to a theory are rare by comparison to the large majority of "passive carriers" (1973, p. 130). The latter, having learned the theory during their graduate training, continue teaching it to others without contributing to its research efforts.

5. Of course, it is entirely possible that *additional* promising students or faculty at these more recent training centers, many of whom have already written one PCT publication, may go on to become contributors in the coming years. My analysis of the importance of the various networks necessarily is biased against those of more recent origin.

6. This prediction of future development in the Florida cluster is based on Mullins's (1973) assertion that a minimum of seven contemporaneous researchers (at least three of whom must be faculty) is needed to produce a stable training and research center, one that can survive the loss of an important member.

7. Since 1980 a third and very active offshoot of this network has emerged in the Department of Communications at the University of Kentucky, where James Applegate, Howard Sypher, and Beverly Davenport-Sypher have collaborated on research in a constructivist theory of communication, extending Crockett and Delia's seminal work in cognitive complexity. See, for example, Applegate (1982), Applegate & Delia (1980), Davenport-Sypher & Sypher (1981), and Sypher & Applegate (1982).

Chapter 4

1. Whether construct theory really is compatible with such a philosophical compromise is open to dispute. Mair and Radley, among others, stress that the truest *implications* of Kelly's thought—not always articulated or realized by Kelly himself—point the way toward a radical reconceptualization of the nature of various forms of human knowing, including scientific inquiry. I shall revisit this issue at a later point.

2. The success of this work was important for another reason as well; it established Academic Press as the major publisher of later PCT work by British authors and editors (i.e., Bannister, 1970, 1977; Fransella & Bannister, 1977; Fransella, 1978; Stringer & Bannister, 1979).

Chapter 5

1. At the time of this work, several other international centers for personal construct work are crystallizing, typically through the efforts of one or two contributors to the theory at each location. Examples include the University of

Capetown, South Africa, where Peter du Preez has been joined by Andy Dawes, whose interests include the personal construct treatment of drug dependence (Dawes, 1985), and the University of Leuven, Belgium, where Omer van den Berg, Paul de Boeck, and William Claeys (1985) are collaborating on PCT research into schizophrenia.

Chapter 6

1. Kelly's personal correspondence indicates that as of July 2, 1964, the Magpie List was founded with sixty-two members. It expanded quickly, doubling in size over the next three years.

2. Bannister's role in maintaining the nascent group was acknowledged by Warren, who wrote in the introduction to the *Proceedings:*

> Gratitude is due to Don Bannister, who in a very real sense made feasible a seminar such as this. With his enthusiasm and wit, and by his chosen function as the hub of a communication network in Britain, Don has initiated and sustained contact between numerous psychologists in different places who might otherwise have felt themselves alone in their interest in Kelly. Thus he made it possible for us to forecast with some certainty that a seminar on Kelly would not lack for support and would fill a definite need. (Warren, 1964, p. 2)

Chapter 7

1. Updated through 1983.

2. Declining the *JASP* editorship, Kelly offered instead to devise and edit a publication entitled *The Ten Worst Journal Papers of the Year*. Needless to say, his offer was refused. While Kelly was making a comment (with characteristically derisive humor) about the rigidity he perceived in mainstream journals, his decision nonetheless impeded the institutionalization of PCT work in established outlets.

3. The difficulty that the American group has had in attaining "elite" status within the parent discipline is reflected in the lead line of Wiley's advertisement for the Landfield and Leitner (1980) book. It reads, "See the implications of this controversial theory. . . ." While copy of this sort undoubtedly is calculated to boost sales, it also mirrors the image PCT still has (after twenty-five years!) in the American psychological community.

Chapter 8

1. I would like to express my appreciation to the following persons, who granted me interviews or responded in writing to the interview questions. *From the United States:* J. Bieri, W. Crockett, R. Cromwell, F. Epting, A. W. Land-

field, L. Leitner, J. Mancuso, G. Neimeyer, and S. Rosenberg. *From Great Britain:* D. Bannister, S. Duck, F. Fransella, R. Holland, J. M. M. Mair, A. Radley, A. Ravenette, D. Rowe, A. Ryle, P. Salmon, P. Slater, and P. Stringer. *From the Netherlands:* H. Bonarius, P. Dingemans, and P. Rathod. *From Canada:* J. R. Adams-Webber. *From Hong Kong:* M. McCoy. Copies of the questions used to structure these interviews, as well as the letter sent to solicit participation, may be obtained from the author.

2. Mancuso and Adams-Webber's edited volume, *The Construing Person* (1982), represents a major attempt to bring the methods and findings of modern cognitive psychology to bear on the basic framework of construct theory. See particularly the chapters by Mancuso and Adams-Webber (on memory and attentional processes), Gara (on the study of prototypes), Crockett (on schemata), Adams-Webber (on information theory and linguistic marking), and Mancuso and Eimer (on features analysis). In a similar vein, I have found that studies of "the self as a cognitive prototype" are immensely suggestive for a personal construct conceptualization of depression and suicide (R. A. Neimeyer, 1984b).

3. For detailed discussion of repertory grid technique and illustrative applications, see Bannister and Mair (1968), Fransella and Bannister (1977), and Neimeyer and Neimeyer (1981).

4. My recommendation that construct theorists end their faithful marriage to the grid and become more methodologically promiscuous is in line with P. Feyerabend's (1978) argument that science is an essentially *anarchistic* enterprise. In essence, he argues that methodological prescriptions stultify, rather than advance, scientific progress, and that the only principle that does not inhibit such progress is: *Anything goes.*

5. Of course, assessing the compatibility of cognitive therapeutic and personal construct approaches is *quite* important in its own right. In other writings (R. A. Neimeyer, 1984a, 1984b; Neimeyer & Neimeyer, 1981a) I have argued that although construct theory *does* differ in certain theoretical respects from many of the cognitive therapies, it is certainly related closely enough to them to permit cross-fertilization. In fact, the two theory groups already share a common interface, an interest in basic experimental work in cognitive psychology. Compare Merluzzi, Rudy, and Glass (1981), representing cognitive therapy, and Ryle (1982) and Mancuso and Adams-Webber (1982) representing construct theory.

6. We need not accept this debate concerning the metatheoretical incompatibilities of the two approaches at face value. As Ben-David (1978, p. 211) observes:

> The relationship to other groups working in the same or related areas will often be determined by competition for scarce resources and rewards (such as recognition, appointments to positions, research grants, or honors). . . . Especially in nonexpanding systems, this competition may lead to conflicts, such as attempts by the

well-established groups to suppress new ones, or attempts by the new groups to overthrow well-established ones. Although in the large majority of cases the conflict is over resources and rewards, and not about mutually exclusive explanations of the same phenomena, such groups will often try to present their views as a contradiction and refutation of those of competing groups and thus justify their claims for withholding rewards and resources from the latter.

REFERENCES

Adams-Webber, J. R. (1970a). An analysis of the discriminant validity of several repertory grid indices. *British Journal of Psychology, 61*, 83–90.

Adams-Webber, J. R. (1970b). Elicited versus provided constructs in repertory grid technique: A review. *British Journal of Medical Psychology, 43*, 349–354.

Adams-Webber, J. R. (1977). The golden section and the structure of self-concepts. *Perceptual and Motor Skills*, 703–706.

Adams-Webber, J. R. (1979). *Personal construct theory: Concepts and applications*. Chichester: John Wiley.

Adams-Webber, J. R. & Mancuso, J. (Eds.). (1983). *Applications of personal construct theory*. Don Mills, Ontario: Academic.

Appelbaum, S. A. (1969). The accidental emminence of George Kelly. *Psychiatry and Social Science Review, 3*, 20–25.

Applebee, A. N. (1975). Developmental changes in consensus in construing within a specified domain. *British Journal of Psychology, 66*, 473–480.

Applebee, A. N. (1976). The development of children's responses to repertory grids. *British Journal of Social and Clinical Psychology, 15*, 101–102.

Applegate, J. L. (1982). The impact of construct system development on communication and impression formation in persuasive contexts. *Communication Monographs, 49*, 277–289.

Applegate, J. L. & Delia, J. G. (1980). Person-centered speech, psychological development, and the contexts of language usage. In R. N. St. Clair and H. Giles (Eds.), *Social and psychological contexts of Language*. Hillsdale, N.J.: Lawrence Erlbaum.

Bandura, A. (1977). Self-efficacy: Toward a unifying theory of behavioral change. *Psychological Review, 84,* 191–215.

Bannister, D. (1960). Conceptual structure in thought disordered schizophrenics. *Journal of Mental Science, 106,* 1230–1249.

Bannister, D. (1962). The nature and measurement of schizophrenic thought disorder. *Journal of Mental Science, 108,* 825–842.

Bannister, D. (1963). A genesis of schizophrenic thought disorder: A serial invalidation of hypothesis. *British Journal of Psychiatry, 109,* 680–686.

Bannister, D. (1965). The genesis of schizophrenic thought disorder: Re-test of the serial invalidation hypothesis. *British Journal of Psychiatry, 111,* 377–382.

Bannister, D. (1969). The myth of physiological psychology. *Bulletin of the British Psychological Society, 21,* 229–231.

Bannister, D. (1970a). Comments on Eysenck's position. In R. Borger & F. Cioffi (Eds.), *Explanation in the behavioral sciences: Confrontations.* London: Cambridge University Press.

Bannister, D. (1970b). *Perspectives in personal construct theory.* London: Academic Press.

Bannister, D. (1970c). Science through the looking glass. In D. Bannister (Ed.), *Perspectives in personal construct theory.* London: Academic Press.

Bannister, D. (1975). Personal construct theory psychotherapy. In D. Bannister (Ed.), *Issues and approaches in the psychological therapies.* London: Wiley.

Bannister, D. (1976). Grid test of thought disorder. *British Journal of Psychiatry, 129,* 93.

Bannister, D. (1977a). *New perspectives in personal construct theory.* London: Academic Press.

Bannister, D. (1977b). The logic of passion. In D. Bannister (Ed.), *New perspectives in personal construct theory.* London: Academic Press.

Bannister, D. (1979). Personal construct theory and politics. In P. Stringer & D. Bannister (Eds.), *Constructs of sociality and individuality.* London: Academic Press.

Bannister, D. (Ed.). (1984). *Further perspectives in personal construct theory.* London: Academic.

Bannister, D., Adams-Webber, J. R., Penn, W. I. & Radley, A. R. (1975). Reversing the process of thought disorder: A serial validation experiment. *British Journal of Social and Clinical Psychology, 14,* 169–180.

Bannister, D. & Agnew, J. (1977). The child's construing of self. In A. Landfield (Ed.), *Nebraska Symposium on Motivation* (Vol. 24). Lincoln: University of Nebraska Press.

Bannister, D. & Fransella, F. (1965). A repertory grid test of schizophrenic thought disorder. *British Journal of Social and Clinical Psychology, 2,* 95–102.

Bannister, D. & Fransella, F. (1967). *Grid test of schizophrenic thought disorder: Manual.* Barnstaple, Devon: Psychological Test Publications.

Bannister, D. & Fransella, F. (1971). *Inquiring man: The theory of personal constructs.* Harmondsworth, England: Penguin.

Bannister, D., Fransella, F. & Agnew, J. (1971). The characteristics and validity of the grid test of thought disorder. *British Journal of Social and Clinical Psychology, 2,* 144–151.

Bannister, D. & Mair, M. (1968). *The evaluation of personal constructs.* London: Academic Press.

Bannister, D. & Salmon, P. (1966). Schizophrenic thought disorder: Specific or diffuse? *British Journal of Medical Psychology, 39,* 215–219.

Bannister, D., Salmon, P. & Lieberman, D. (1964). Diagnosis—treatment relationships in psychiatry: a statistical analysis. *British Journal of Psychiatry, 110,* 726–732.

Bavelas, J., Chan, A. & Guthrie, J. (1976). Reliability and validity of traits measured by Kelly's repertory grid. *Canadian Journal of Behavioral Science, 8,* 1, 23–38.

Beard, R. (1978). Teachers' and pupils' construing of reading. In F. Fransella (Ed.), *Personal construct psychology 1977.* New York: Academic.

Beck, A. T. (1970). Cognitive therapy: Nature and relation to behavior therapy. *Behavior Therapy, 1,* 184–200.

Beck, A. T., Rush, J., Shaw, B., & Emery, G. (1979). *Cognitive therapy of depression.* New York: Guilford.

Becker, H. A. (1981). The four demons chasing the social scientist. In H. Bonarius, R. Holland & S. Rosenberg (Eds.), *Personal construct psychology: Recent advances in theory and practice.* London: Macmillan.

Ben-David, J. (1978). Emergence of national traditions in the sociology of science. In J. Gaston (Ed.), *Sociology of science,* San Francisco: Jossey-Bass.

Benjafield, J. & Adams-Webber, J. R. (1976). The golden section hypothesis. *British Journal of Psychology, 67,* 1.

Benjafield, J. & Green, T. R. G. (1978). Golden section relations in interpersonal judgment. *British Journal of Psychology, 69,* 25–35.

Bieri, J. (1955). Cognitive complexity-simplicity and predictive behavior. *Journal of Abnormal and Social Psychology, 51,* 263–268.

Bishop, F. & Kelly, G. A. (1942). A projective method of personality investigation. *Psychological Bulletin, 39,* 599.

Bloor, D. (1976). *Knowledge and social imagery.* London: Rontledge & Kegan Paul.

Bonarius, H. (1971). *Personal construct theory and extreme response style: An interaction model of meaningfulness, maladjustment, and communication.* Amsterdam: Swets & Zeitlinger.

Bonarius, H. (1977). The interaction model of communication: Through experimental research towards existential relevance. In A. Landfield (Ed.),

Nebraska Symposium on Motivation (Vol. 24). Lincoln: University of Nebraska Press.

Bonarius, H. (1980). *Persoonlijke psychologie. Deel II*. Van Loghum Slaterus.

Bonarius, H., Holland, R. & Rosenberg, S. (Eds.). (1981). *Personal construct psychology: Recent advances in theory and practice*. London: Macmillan.

Bonarius, J. C. J. (1965). Research in the personal construct theory of George A. Kelly. In B. Maher (Ed.), *Progress in experimental personality research*, Vol. II. New York: Academic Press.

Bonarius, J. C. J. (1967a). Extreme beoordelingen en persoonlijke constructen: een vergelijking van verschillende indices van extremeit. *Hypothese, 12*, 46–57.

Bonarius, J. C. J. (1967b). The fixed role therapy of George A. Kelly. *Nederlands Tijdschrift voor Psychologie en Haar Grensgebieden, 22*, 482–520.

Bonarius, J. C. J. (June 1968). Personal constructs and extremity of ratings. *Heyman Bulletins*.

Bonarius, J. C. J. (1970). Fixed role therapy: A double paradox. *British Journal of Medical Psychology, 43*, 213–219.

Borgo, S., Liotti, G., & Sibilia, L. (1973). Conceptual models in psychiatry. *Rivista di Psichiatria, 8*, 262–275.

Bruner, J. S. (1956). You are your constructs. *Contemporary Psychology, 1*, 355–357.

Bruner, J. S. & Postman, L. (1949). Perception, cognition, and behavior. *Journal of Personality, 18*, 15–31.

Canter, D. V. (1968). Should we treat building users as subjects or objects? In D. Canter (Ed.), *Architecture of psychology*. Conference at Strathclyde.

Canter, D. V. (1974). *Psychology for architects*. London: Applied Science Publishers.

Caplan, H. L., Rohde, P. D., Shapiro, D. A. & Watson, J. P. (1975). Some correlates of repertory grid measures used to study a psychotherapeutic group. *British Journal of Medical Psychology, 48*, 217–226.

Catina, A. & Marcus, S. (1976). Appreciative style and art perception: II. *Revista de Psihologie, 22*, 395–403.

Cautela, J. R. (1967). Covert sensitization. *Psychological Reports, 20*, 459–468.

Chetwynd, S. J. (1976). Sex differences in stereotyping the roles of wife and mother. In P. Slater (Ed.), *Explorations of Intrapersonal space*. London: Wiley.

Cochran, L. R. (1976). Categorization and change in conceptual relatedness. *Canadian Journal of Behavioural Science, 8*, 275–286.

Cochran, L. R. (1977). Differences between supplied and elicited considerations in career evaluation. *Social Behavior and Personality, 5*, 241–247.

Collett, P. (1979). The repertory grid in psychological research. In G. P. Ginsburg (Ed.), *Emerging strategies in social psychological research*. Chichester: Wiley.

Collins, H. M. & Pinch, T. J. (1978). The construction of the paranormal: Nothing unscientific is happening. In R. Wallis (Ed.), *Rejected knowledge*. Keele: University of Keele Press.

Crane, D. (1972). *Invisible colleges: Diffusion of knowledge in scientific communities*. Chicago: University of Chicago Press.

Crisp, A. H. (1964a). Development and application of a measure of "transference." *Journal of Psychosomatic Research*, 8, 327–335.

Crisp, A. H. (1964b). An attempt to measure an aspect of "transference." *British Journal of Medical Psychology*, 37, 17–30.

Crisp, A. H. & Fransella, F. (1972). Conceptual changes during recovery from anorexia nervosa. *British Journal of Medical Psychology*, 45, 395–405.

Crockett, W. H. (1982). The organization of construct systems. In J. Mancuso & J. R. Adams-Webber (Eds.), *The construing person*. New York: Praeger.

Crockett, W. H., Gonyea, A. H. & Delia, J. G. (1970). Cognitive complexity and the formation of impression from abstract qualities or from concrete behavior. *Proceedings of the Annual Convention of the American Psychological Association*, 5, 357–376.

Cromwell, R. L. & Caldwell, D. F. (1962). A comparison of ratings based on personal constructs of self and others. *Journal of Clinical Psychology*, 18, 43–46.

Davenport-Sypher, B. & Sypher, H. E. (1981). Individual differences and perceptions of communication abilities in an organizational setting. Paper presented at the Annual Meeting of the International Communication Association, Minneapolis.

Davisson, A. (1978). George Kelly and the American mind. In F. Fransella (Ed.), *Personal construct psychology, 1977*. New York: Academic Press.

Dawes, A. (1985). Drug dependence. In E. Button (Ed.), *Personal construct theory and mental health*. London: Croom Helm.

Delia, J. G., Crockett, W. H., Press, A. N. & O'Keefe, D. J. (1975). The dependency of interpersonal evaluations on context-relevant beliefs about the other. *Speech Monographs*, 42, 10–19.

Dingemans, P. M. (1980). Shizofrenie-onderzoek vanuit de theorie van persoonlijke constructen. *Nederland Tijdschrift voor de Psychologie*, 35, 345.

Dingemans, P. M., Space, L. G. & Cromwell, R. L. (1983). How general is the inconsistency in schizophrenic behavior? In J. R. Adams-Webber and J. Mancuso (Eds.), *Applications of personal construct theory*. Don Mills, Ontario: Academic.

Dolliver, R. H. & Woodward, B. T. (1975). A note on reflexivity in personality theories. *Journal of Individual Psychology*, 31, 18–22.

Duck, S. W. (1973). *Personal relationships and personal constructs*. London: Wiley.

Duck, S. W. (1975). Personality similarity and friendship choices by adolescents. *European Journal of Social Psychology*, 5, 351–365.

Duck, S. W. (1977). Inquiry, hypothesis and the quest for validation: Personal construct systems in the development of acquaintance. In S. Duck (Ed.), *Theory and practice in interpersonal attraction*. London: Academic Press.

Duck, S. W. (1979). The personal and the interpersonal in construct theory: Social and individual aspects of relationships. In P. Stringer & D. Bannister (Eds.), *Constructs of sociality and individuality*. London: Academic.

Duck, S. W. & Allison, D. (1978). I liked you but I can't live with you: A study of lapsed relationships. *Social Behavior and Personality, 6*, 43–47.

Duck, S. W. & Craig, G. (1977). The relative attractiveness of different types of information about another person. *British Journal of Social and Clinical Psychology, 15*, 229–233.

Duck, S. W. & Craig, G. (1978). Personality similarity and the development of friendship: A longitudinal study. *British Journal of Social and Clinical Psychology, 17*, 237–242.

Duck, S. W. & Miell, D. E. (1981). Towards an understanding of relationship development and breakdown. In H. Tajfel (Ed.), *The social dimension*. Cambridge: Cambridge University Press.

Duck, S. W., Miell, D. K. & Gaebler, H. C. (1980). Attraction and communication in children's interactions. In H. Foot, A. Chapman & J. Smith (Eds.), *Friendship and childhood relationships*. London: Wiley.

Duck, S. W. & Spencer, C. (1972). Personal constructs and friendship formation. *Journal of Personality and Social Psychology, 23*, 40–45.

du Preez, P. (1972). The construction of alternatives in parliamentary debate: Psychological theory and political analysis. *South African Journal of Psychology, 2*, 23–40.

du Preez, P. (1975). The application of Kelly's personal construct theory to the analysis of political debates. *Journal of Social Psychology, 95*, 267–270.

du Preez, P. (1979). Politics and identity in South Africa. In P. Stringer & D. Bannister (Eds.), *Constructs of sociality and individuality*. London: Academic Press.

du Preez, P. & Ward, D. G. (1970). Personal constructs of modern and traditional Xhosa. *Journal of Social Psychology, 82*, 149–160.

Eland, F., Epting, F., & Bonarius, H. (1979). Self-disclosure and the reptest interaction technique (RIT). In P. Stringer & D. Bannister (Eds.), *Constructs of sociality and individuality*. London: Academic.

Ellis, A. (1969). A cognitive approach to behavior therapy. *International Journal of Psychotherapy, 8*, 896–900.

Epting, F. R. (1984). *Personal construct theory counseling and psychotherapy*. London: Wiley.

Epting, F. R., & Landfield, A. W. (Eds.). (1985). *Anticipating personal construct theory*. Lincoln: University of Nebraska Press.

Epting, F. R. & Neimeyer, R. A. (Eds.). (1984). *Personal meanings of death: Applications of personal construct theory to clinical practice.* New York: Hemisphere/McGraw-Hill.

Epting, F. R. & Wilkins, G. (1974). Comparison of cognitive structural measures for predicting person perception. *Perceptual and Motor Skills, 38,* 727–730.

Epting, F. R., Zempel, C. E. & Rubio, C. T. (1979). Construct similarity and maternal warmth. *Social Behavior and Personality, 7,* 97–105.

Feyerabend, P. (1978). *Against Method.* London: Verso.

Foulds, G. A. (1973). Has anybody here seen Kelly? *British Journal of Medical Psychology, 46,* 221.

Foulds, G. A. (1976). The real Kelly by McCoy: A rejoinder. *British Journal of Medical Psychology, 49,* 295.

Foulds, G. A., Hope, K., McPherson, F. M. & Mayo, P. R. (1967). Cognitive disorder among the schizophrenias I: The validity of some tests of thought process disorder. *British Journal of Psychiatry, 113,* 1361–1368.

Fransella, F. (1969). The stutterer as subject or object. In B. Gray & G. England (Eds.), *Stuttering and the conditioning therapies.* Monterey, California: Monterey Institute for Speech and Hearing.

Fransella, F. (1970). Stuttering: Not a symptom but a way of life. *British Journal of Disorders of Communication, 5,* 22–29.

Fransella, F. (1972). *Personal change and reconstruction: Research on a treatment of stuttering.* London: Academic Press.

Fransella, F. (1974). Thinking in the obsessional. In H. Beech (Ed.), *Obsessional states.* London: Methuen.

Fransella, F. (1976). The theory and measurement of personal constructs. In K. Granville-Grossman (Ed.), *Recent advances in clinical psychiatry* (Vol. 2). London: Churchill Livingstone.

Fransella, F., (Ed.). (1978a). *Personal construct psychology 1977.* New York: Academic Press.

Fransella, F. (1978b). Personal construct theory or psychology? In F. Fransella (Ed.), *Personal construct psychology 1977.* New York: Academic Press.

Fransella, F. (1980). Teaching personal construct psychology. In A. Landfield & L. Leitner (Eds.), *Personal construct theory: Psychotherapy and personality.* New York: Wiley.

Fransella, F. & Bannister, D. (1977). *A manual for repertory grid technique.* London: Academic Press.

Fransella, F. & Crisp, A. H. (1970). Conceptual organisation and weight change. *Psychotherapy and Psychosomatics, 18,* 176–185.

Fransella, F. & Crisp, A. H. (1979). Comparisons of weight concepts in groups of neurotic, normal, and anorexic females. *British Journal of Psychiatry, 134,* 79–86.

Frost, W. A. K. & Braine, R. L. (1967). The application of the repertory grid technique to problems in market research. *Commentary*, 9, 161–175.

Goldfried, M. & Merbaum, M. (Eds.). (1973). *Behavior change through self-control*. New York: Holt, Rinehart and Winston.

Griffith, B. C. & Mullins, N. C. (1972). Coherent groups in scientific change: 'Invisible Colleges' may be consistent throughout science. *Science*, 177, 959–964.

Guidano, V. & Liotti, G. (1983). *Cognitive processes and emotional disorders*. New York: Guilford.

Harri-Augstein, E. S. (1978). Reflecting on structure of meaning: A process of learning to learn. In F. Fransella (Ed.), *Personal Construct Psychology 1977*. New York: Academic Press.

Harrison, A. & Phillips, J. P. N. (1979). The specificity of schizophrenic thought disorder. *British Journal of Medical Psychology*, 52, 105–117.

Harrison, J. & Sarre, P. (1971). Personal construct theory in the measurement of environmental images: Problems and methods. *Environment and Behavior*, 3, 351–374.

Harrison, J. & Sarre, P. (1975). Personal construct theory in the measurement of environmental images. *Environment and Behavior*, 7, 3–58.

Harrison, J. & Sarre, P. (1976). Personal construct theory, the repertory grid, and environmental cognition. In G. Moore & R. Gollege (Eds.), *Environmental knowing: Theories, research and methods*. Stroudsberg, Penn.: Dowden, Hutchison & Ross.

Heather, N. (1976). The specificity of schizophrenic thought disorder: A replication and extension of previous findings. *British Journal of Social and Clinical Psychology*, 15, 131–137.

Heather, N., McPherson, F. M. & Sprent, P. (1978). The analysis of interactions in experiments on the specificity of schizophrenic thought disorder: A reply to Phillips. *British Journal of Social and Clinical Psychology*, 17, 379–382.

Holland, R. (1970). George Kelly: Constructive innocent and reluctant existentialist. In D. Bannister (Ed.), *Perspectives in personal construct theory*. London: Academic Press.

Holland, R. (1977). *Self and social context*. London: St. Martins.

Holland, R. (1979). From perspectives to reflexivity. Paper presented at the Third International Congress on Personal Construct Psychology, Breukelen, the Netherlands.

Holland, R. (1981). From perspectives to reflexivity. In H. Bonarius, R. Holland & S. Rosenberg (Eds.), *Personal construct psychology: Recent advances in theory and practice*. London: Macmillan.

Howard, A. R. & Kelly, G. A. (1954). A theoretical approach to psychological movement. *Journal of Abnormal and Social Psychology*, 49, 399–404.

Inhaber, H. (1977). Where scientists publish. *Social Studies of Science, 7,* 388–394.

Kelly, G. A. (1924). The sincere motive. *Messenger of Peace, 49,* 76–80.

Kelly, G. A. (1933). Some observations on the relation of cerebral dominance to the perception of symbols. *Psychological Bulletin, 30,* 583–584.

Kelly, G. A. (1938). A method of diagnosing personality in the psychological clinic. *Psychological Record, 2,* 95–111.

Kelly, G. A. (1940). Some practical considerations in the formulation of clinical recommendations. *Psychological Bulletin, 37,* 576.

Kelly, G. A. (1945a). War weariness in U.S. Naval aviation. A series of classified reports for the Deputy Chief of Naval Operations (Air), U.S. Navy.

Kelly, G. A. (1945b). Perceptual integration in the design of aircraft instrument panels. Report to Aviation Psychology Branch, Division of Aviation Medicine, Bureau of Medicine and Surgery, U.S. Navy.

Kelly, G. A. (Ed.). (1945c. Issued 1947). *New methods in applied psychology.* Report of the 1945 Conference on Military Psychology. College Park, Md.: University of Maryland.

Kelly, G. A. (1946). Standardization of technique in clinical psychology. Unpublished manuscript, University of Maryland.

Kelly, G. A. (1951). Training for professional function in clinical psychology. *American Journal of Orthopsychiatry, 21,* 312–318.

Kelly, G. A. (1955). *The psychology of personal constructs* (Vols. I and II). New York: Norton.

Kelly, G. A. (1963). *A theory of personality.* New York: Norton.

Kelly, G. A. (1969). Ontological acceleration. In B. Maher (Ed.), *Clinical psychology and personality: The selected papers of George Kelly.* New York: Wiley & Sons.

Kendall, P. C. (Ed.). (1985). *Advances in Cognitive-behavioral research and therapy.* New York: Academic.

Kendall, P. C. & Hollon, S. D. (1979). Cognitive-behavioral interventions: Overview and current status. In P. Kendall & S. Hollon (Eds.), *Cognitive-behavioral interventions.* New York: Academic.

Kuhn, T. (1962). *The structure of scientific revolutions.* Chicago: University of Chicago Press.

Kuhn, T. S. (1970). *The structure of scientific revolutions, 2nd edition.* Chicago: University of Chicago Press.

Kuusinen, J. & Nystedt, L. (1975). The convergent validity of four indices of cognitive complexity in person perception: A multi-index multimethod and factor analytical approach. *Scandinavian Journal of Psychology, 15,* 131–136.

Lakatos, I. (1978). *The methodology of scientific research programs.* Cambridge: Cambridge University Press.

Landfield, A. W. (1954). A movement interpretation of threat. *Journal of Abnormal Social Psychology*, 49, 529–532.

Landfield, A. W. (1971). *Personal construct systems in psychotherapy*. Chicago: Rand McNally.

Landfield, A. W. (Ed.). (1977). *Nebraska Symposium on Motivation* (Vol. 24). Lincoln: University of Nebraska Press.

Landfield, A. W. (1979). Exploring socialization through the interpersonal transaction group. In P. Stringer & D. Bannister (Eds.), *Constructs of sociality and individuality*. London: Academic Press.

Landfield, A. W. (1980). Personal construct psychology: A theory to be elaborated. In M. Mahoney (Ed.), *Psychotherapy process*. New York: Plenum.

Landfield, A. W. & Allee, R. (1966). Twelve case reports examined in terms of Shaw's Reconciliation Theory. *Psychotherapy: Theory, Research and Practice*, 3, 125–134.

Landfield, A. W. & Leitner, L. M. (1980). *Personal construct theory: Psychotherapy and personality*. New York: Wiley.

Leitner, L. M. (1981). Psychopathology and the differentiation of values, emotions and behaviors: A repertory grid study. *British Journal of Psychiatry*, 138, 147–153.

Lemaine, G., MacLeod, R., Mulkay, M. & Weingart, P. (1976). *Perspectives on the emergence of scientific disciplines*. Chicago: Aldine.

Lemaine, G., Weingart, P., Mulkay, M. & Edge, D. (1976). Introduction. In G. Lemaine, et al. (Eds.), *Perspectives on the emergence of scientific disciplines*. Chicago: Aldine.

Lemon, N. (1975). Linguistic development and conceptualisation: a bilingual study. *Journal of Cross-Cultural Psychology*, 6, 173–188.

Lemon, N. (1976). Linguistic factors and meaningfulness of personal constructs. *European Journal of Social Psychology*, 6, 71–80.

Lemon, N. & Warren, N. (1974). Salience, centrality and self-relevance of traits in construing others. *British Journal of Social and Clinical Psychology*, 13, 119–124.

Lifshitz, M. (1973). Girls' identification with their fathers—a key to striving of equality. *Social Research Review*, 4, 69–76.

Lifshitz, M. (1974). Social differentiation and integration of fatherless adolescents. *Magamot*, 20, 347–372.

Lifshitz, M. (1975a). Social differentiation and organization of the Rorschach in fatherless and two-parented children. *Journal of Clinical Psychology*, 31, 126–130.

Lifshitz, M. (1975b). Long range effects of father's loss: The cognitive complexity of bereaved children and their school adjustment. *British Journal of Medical Psychology*, 49, 189–197.

Lifshitz, M. (1978). Girls' identity formation as related to perception of parents. *Social Behavior and Personality*, 6, 81–88.

Lifshitz, M. & Ben-Tuvia, S. (1975). The effect of fatherlessness versus two-parented family structure upon preadolescents' perceptual differentiation and social behavior. *International Mental Health Research Newsletter.*

Lifshitz, M., Reznikov, R. & Aran, M. (1974). Adjustment of kibbutz children as a reflection of the degree of similarity between parents. *Studies in Education*, 5, 107–118.

Little, B. R. (1968). Psychospecialization: Functions of differential interest in persons and things. *Bulletin of the British Psychological Society*, 21, 113.

Little, B. R. (1977). Review of Patrick Slater's Explorations of Intrapersonal Space, Vol. I. *Contemporary Psychology*, 22, 759–761.

Little, B. R. & Kane, M. (1974). Person-thing orientation and privacy. *Man-Environment Systems*, 4, 361–364.

Maher, B. A. (1969). *Clinical psychology and personality: The selected papers of George Kelly.* New York: Wiley.

Mahoney, M. (1974). *Cognition and behavior modification.* Cambridge, Mass.: Ballinger.

Mahoney, M. (Ed.). (1980). *Psychotherapy process.* New York: Plenum.

Mahoney, M. & Arnkoff, D. (1978). Cognitive and self-control therapies. In S. Garfield & A. Bergin (Eds.), *Handbook of psychotherapy and behavior change.* (2nd ed.), New York: Wiley.

Mair, J. M. M. (1966). Prediction of grid scores. *British Journal of Psychology*, 57, 187–192.

Mair, J. M. M. (1967). Some problems in repertory grid measurement: I. The use of bipolar constructs. *British Journal of Psychology*, 58, 261–270.

Mair, J. M. M. (1970a). The person in psychology and psychotherapy: An introduction. *British Journal of Medical Psychology*, 43, 197–205.

Mair, J. M. M. (1970b). Psychologists are human too. In D. Bannister (Ed.), *Perspectives in personal construct theory.* London: Academic.

Mair, J. M. M. (1977a). Metaphors for living. In A. Landfield (Ed.), *Nebraska Symposium on Motivation* (Vol. 24). Lincoln: University of Nebraska Press.

Mair, J. M. M. (1977b). The community of self. In D. Bannister (Ed.), *New perspectives in personal construct theory.* London: Academic.

Mair, J. M. M. (1979). The personal venture. In P. Stringer & D. Bannister (Eds.), *Constructs of sociality and individuality.* London: Academic.

Mair, J. M. M. & Crisp, A. H. (1968). Estimating psychological organization, meaning, and change in relation to clinical practice. *British Journal of Medical Psychology*, 41, 15–29.

Maklouf, M. F., Jones, H. G. & Norris, H. (1970). Articulation of the conceptual structure in obsessional neurosis. *British Journal of Social and Clinical Psychology*, 9, 264–274.

Makhlouf-Norris, F. & Jones, H. G. (1971). Conceptual distance indices as measures of alienation in obsessional neurosis. *Psychological Medicine*, 5, 381–387.

Makhlouf-Norris, F. & Norris, H. (1973). The obsessive compulsive syndrome as a neurotic device for the reduction of self-uncertainty. *British Journal of Psychiatry*, 122, 277–288.

Mancuso, J. C. (1977). Current motivational models in the elaboration of personal construct theory. In A. Landfield (Ed.), *Nebraska Symposium on Motivation* (Vol. 24). Lincoln: University of Nebraska Press.

Mancuso, J. C. & Adams-Webber, J. R. (1982). *The construing person*. New York: Praeger.

Mancuso, J. C. & Handin, K. (1980). Training parents to construe their child's construing. In A. Landfield & L. Leitner (Eds.), *Personal construct theory: Psychotherapy and personality*. New York: Wiley.

Marcus, S. & Catina, A. (1976, 1977). Appreciative style and art perception. *Revue Roumaine des Sciences Sociales; Serie de Psychologie*. (I) 20, 65–74; (II) 21, 79–86.

McArthur, C. Review of Kelly, G. A. (1956). The psychology of personal constructs. *Journal of Counseling Psychology*, 3, 306–307.

McCoy, M. M. (1975). Foulds's phenomenological windmill: A reply to criticisms of personal construct psychology. *British Journal of Medical Psychology*, 48, 139–146.

McCoy, M. M. (1977). A reconstruction of emotion. In D. Bannister (Ed.), *New perspectives in personal construct theory*. London: Academic.

McCoy, M. M. (1980). Culture-shocked marriages. In A. Landfield & L. Leitner (Eds.), *Personal construct theory: Psychotherapy and personality*. New York: Wiley.

McCoy, M. M. (1981). Positive and negative emotion: A personal construct theory interpretation. In H. Bonarius, R. Holland & S. Rosenberg (Eds.), *Personal construct psychology: Recent advances in theory and practice*. London: Macmillan.

McFayden, M. & Foulds, G. A. (1972). Comparison of provided and elicited grid content in the grid test of schizophrenic thought disorder. *British Journal of Psychiatry*, 121, 53–57.

McPherson, F. M. (1969). Thought-process disorder, delusions of persecution and "non-integration" in schizophrenia. *British Journal of Medical Psychology*, 42, 55–57.

McPherson, F. M. (1972). "Psychological" constructs and "psychological" symptoms in schizophrenia. *British Journal of Psychiatry*, 120, 197–198.

McPherson, F. M., Armstrong, J. & Heather, N. (1975). Psychological construing, difficulty and thought disorder. *British Journal of Medical Psychology*, 48, 303–315.

McPherson, F. M., Bardon, V. & Buckley, F. (1970). The uses of psychological constructs by affectively flattened schizophrenics. *British Journal of Medical Psychology, 43,* 291–293.

McPherson, F. M., Bardon, V., Hay, J. A. & Kushner, A. W. (1970). Flattening of affect and personal constructs. *British Journal of Psychiatry, 116,* 39–43.

McPherson, F. M., Blackburn, I. M., Draffan, J. W. & McFayden, M. A. (1973). A further study of the grid test of thought disorder. *British Journal of Social and Clinical Psychology, 12,* 420–427.

McPherson, F. M. & Buckley, F. (1970). Thought-process disorder and personal construct subsystems. *British Journal of Social and Clinical Psychology, 9,* 380–381.

McPherson, F. M., Buckley, F. & Draffan, J. (1971). "Psychological" constructs, thought-process disorder and flattening of affect. *British Journal of Social and Clinical Psychology, 10,* 267–270.

McPherson, F. M. & Walton, H. J. (1970). The dimensions of psychotherapy group interactions: An analysis of clinicians' constructs. *British Journal of Medical Psychology, 43,* 281–290.

Meichenbaum, D. (1974). *Cognitive behavior modification.* Morristown, N.J.: General Learning Press.

Mellsop, G. W., Spellman, M. S. & Harrison, A. W. (1971). The performance of manic patients on the grid-test for schizophrenic thought disorder. *British Journal of Psychiatry, 118,* 671–673.

Merleau-Ponty, M. (1967). *Phenomenology of perception.* London: Routledge & Kegan Paul.

Merluzzi, T., Glass, C. & Genest, M. (Eds.). (1981). *Cognitive assessment.* New York: Guilford.

Merluzzi, T., Rudy, T. & Glass, C. (1981). The information-processing paradigm. Implications for clinical science. In T. Merluzzi, C. Glass & M. Genest (Eds.), *Cognitive Assessment.* New York: Guilford.

Meshoulom, U. (1978). There is more to stuttering than meets the ear: Stutters' construing of speaking situations. In F. Fransella (Ed.), *Personal construct psychology 1977.* New York: Academic Press.

Miller, A. (1978). Conceptual systems theory: A critical review. *Genetic Psychology Monographs, 97,* 77–126.

Miller, A. & Wilson, P. (1979). Cognitive differentiation and integration: A conceptual analysis. *Genetic Psychology Monographs, 99,* 3–40.

Millstone, E. (1978). A framework for sociology of knowledge. *Social Studies of Science, 8,* 111–125.

Mischel, W. (1981). Personality and cognition: Something borrowed, something new? In N. Cantor & J. F. Kihlstrom (Eds.), *Personality, cognition and social interaction.* Hillsdale, N.J.: Erlbaum.

Moss, A. E. (1974a). Shakespeare and role-construct therapy. *British Journal of Medical Psychology, 47,* 235–252.

Moss, A. E. (1974b). Hamlet and role-construct theory. *British Journal of Medical Psychology, 47,* 253–264.

Mulkay, M. J. (1976). Methodology in the sociology of science: Some reflections on the study of radio astronomy. In G. Lemaine, et al. (Eds.), *Perspectives on the emergence of scientific disciplines.* Chicago: Aldine.

Mulkay, M. J. (1979). *Science and the sociology of knowledge.* London: George Allen & Urwin.

Mullins, N. C. (1972). The development of a scientific speciality: The Phage Group and the origins of molecular biology. *Minerva, 10,* 51–82.

Mullins, N. C. (1973). *Theories and theory groups in contemporary American sociology.* New York: Harper & Row.

Neimeyer, G. J., Banikiotes, P. G. & Ianni, L. E. (1979). Self-disclosure and psychological construing: A personal construct approach to interpersonal perceptions. *Social Behavior and Personality, 7,* 161–165.

Neimeyer, G. J. & Merluzzi, T. V. (July 1979). Group structure and group process: A personal construct approach to group development. Paper presented at the Third International Congress on Personal Construct Psychology, Breukelen, the Netherlands.

Neimeyer, G. J. & Neimeyer, R. A. (1981a). Personal construct perspectives on cognitive assessment. In T. Merluzzi, C. Glass & M. Genest (Eds.), *Cognitive assessment.* New York: Guilford Press.

Neimeyer, G. J. & Neimeyer, R. A. (1981b). Functional similarity and interpersonal attraction. *Journal of Research in Personality, 15,* 427–435.

Neimeyer, R. A. (March 1977). Knowing and construing: A Kantian analysis of George Kelly's psychology of personal constructs. Paper read at the Third Annual Meeting of the Society for Philosophy and Psychology, University of Pittsburgh.

Neimeyer, R. A. (1980). George Kelly as therapist: A review of his tapes. In A. Landfield & L. Leitner (Eds.), *Personal construct theory: Psychotherapy and personality.* New York: Wiley.

Neimeyer, R. A. (1981). The structure and meaningfulness of tacit construing. In H. Bonarius, R. Holland & S. Rosenberg (Eds.), *Personal construct psychology: Recent advances in theory and practice.* London: Macmillan.

Neimeyer, R. A. (1984a). Towards a personal construct conceptualization of depression and suicide. In F. R. Epting and R. A. Neimeyer (Eds.), *Personal meanings of death: Applications of personal construct theory to clinical practice.* New York: Hemisphere/McGraw-Hill.

Neimeyer, R. A. (1984b). Personal constructs in clinical practice. In P. C. Kendall (Ed.), *Advances in cognitive-behavioral research and therapy.* (Vol. 4). New York: Academic.

Neimeyer, R. A. & Dingemans, P. (1980). Death orientation in the suicide intervention worker. *Omega: Journal of Death and Dying, 11,* 15–23.

Neimeyer, R. A., Dingemans, P. M. & Epting, F. R. (1977). Convergent validity, situation stability, and meaningfulness of the Threat Index. *Omega: Journal of Death and Dying, 8,* 251–265.

Neimeyer, R. A. & Neimeyer, G. J. (1977). A personal construct approach to perception of disclosure targets. *Perceptual and Motor Skills, 44,* 791–794.

Neimeyer, R. A. & Neimeyer, G. J. (1983). Structural similarity in the acquaintance process. *Journal of Social and Clinical Psychology, 1,* 146–154.

Neimeyer, R. A., Heath, A. & Strauss, J. (1985). Personal reconstruction during group cognitive therapy for depression. In F. R. Epting and A. W. Landfield (Eds.), *Anticipating personal construct theory.* Lincoln: University of Nebraska Press.

Norris, H. & Makhlouf-Norris, G. (1976). The measurement of self-identity. In P. Slater (Ed.), *The measurement of intrapersonal space.* (Vol. 1). London: Wiley.

Nystedt, L., Kuusinen, J. & Ekehammar, B. (1976). Structural representations of person perception: A comparison between own and provided constructs. *Scandinavian Journal of Psychology, 17,* 223–233.

O'Donovan, D. (1965). Rating extremity: Pathology or meaningfulness. *Psychology Review, 72,* 358–372.

Oliver, D. W. & Landfield, A. W. (1962). Reflexivity. *Journal of Individual Psychology, 18,* 114–124.

O'Reilly, J. (1977). The interplay between mothers and their children: A construct theory viewpoint. In D. Bannister (Ed.), *New perspectives in personal construct theory.* London: Academic.

Pervin, L. (1973). On construing our constructs. A review of Bannister and Fransella's Inquiring Man: The theory of personal constructs. *Contemporary Psychology, 18,* 110–112.

Phillips, J., Cashdan, A., Flynn, R. & Meadows, S. (1979). Changes over time in nursery school teachers' behavior: A report of a field experimental study. *Bulletin of the British Psychological Society, 32,* 207.

Polanyi, M. (1958). *Personal knowledge.* New York: Harper.

Poole, A. D. (1976). A further attempt to cross-validate the grid test of schizophrenic thought disorder. *British Journal of Social and Clinical Psychology, 15,* 197–188.

Poole, A. D. (1979). The grid test of schizophrenic thought disorder and psychiatric symptomatology. *British Journal of Medical Psychology, 52,* 183–186.

Pope, M. (1978). Monitoring and reflecting in teacher training. In F. Fransella (Ed.), *Personal construct psychology 1977.* New York: Academic.

Pope, M. L. & Keen, T. R. (1981). *Personal construct psychology and education*. London: Academic.

Pope, M. & Shaw, M. (1981). Negotiation in learning. In H. Bonarius, R. Holland, and S. Rosenberg (Eds.), *Personal construct psychology: Recent advances in theory and practice*. London: Macmillan.

Presley, A. S. (1969). "Slowness" and performance on the grid test for thought disorder. *British Journal of Social and Clinical Psychology*, 8, 79–80.

Price, D. J. de S. (1961). *Science since Babylon*. New Haven: Yale University Press.

Radley, A. R. (1974a). Schizophrenic thought disorder and the nature of personal constructs. *British Journal of Social and Clinical Psychology*, 13, 315–327.

Radley, A. R. (1974b). The effect of role enactment upon construed alternatives. *British Journal of Medical Psychology*, 47, 313–320.

Radley, A. R. (1977). Living on the horizon. In D. Bannister (Ed.), *New perspectives in personal construct theory*. London: Academic.

Radley, A. R. (1978a). Deliberation and awareness in personal conduct. *Journal of Phenomenological Psychology*, 8, 63–84.

Radley, A. R. (1978b). The opposing self. In F. Fransella (Ed.), *Personal construct psychology 1977*. London: Academic.

Radley, A. R. (1979). Construing as praxis. In P. Stringer & D. Bannister (Eds.), *Constructs of sociality and individuality*. London: Academic.

Radnitsky, G. (1973). *Contemporary schools of metascience*. Chicago: Gateway.

Rathod, P. (1980). The reliability of the principal components of rep grid data. *Nederlands Tijdschrift voor de Psychologie*, 35, 331–344.

Rathod, P. (1981). Methods for the analysis of rep grid data. In H. Bonarius, R. Holland & S. Rosenberg (Eds.), *Personal construct psychology: Recent advances in theory and practice*. London: Macmillan.

Ravenette, A. T. (1968). *Dimensions of reading difficulties*. Oxford: Pergamon Press.

Ravenette, A. T. (1975). Grid techniques for children. *Journal of Child Psychology and Psychiatry*, 16, 79–83.

Ravenette, A. T. (1977). Personal construct theory: An approach to the psychological investigation of children. In D. Bannister (Ed.), *New perspectives in personal construct theory*. London: Academic.

Ravenette, A. T. (1980). The explanation of consciousness: Personal construct investigation with children. In A. Landfield & L. Leitner (Eds.), *Personal construct psychology: Psychotherapy and personality*. New York: Wiley.

Rigdon, M., Epting, F. R., Neimeyer, R. A. & Krieger, S. R. (1979). The Threat Index: A research report. *Death Education*, 3, 245–270.

Rimm, D. C. & Masters, J. C. (1979). *Behavior Therapy*. New York: Academic.

Robinson, A. J. & Kelly, G. A. (1942). A further validation of role therapy. *Psychological Bulletin*, 39, 596.

Rogers, C. R. (1956). Intellectual psychotherapy. *Contemporary Psychology, 1,* 357–358.

Rowe, D. (1969). Estimates of change in a depressive patient. *British Journal of Psychiatry, 115,* 1,199–1,200.

Rowe, D. (1971a). An examination of a psychiatrist's predictions of a patient's constructs. *British Journal of Psychiatry, 118,* 231–234.

Rowe, D. (1971b). Poor prognosis in a case of depression as predicted by the repertory grid. *British Journal of Psychiatry, 118,* 297–300.

Rowe, D. (1973a). The use of the repertory grid in the study of object relations. *British Journal of Projective Psychology and Personality Study, 18,* 11–19.

Rowe, D. (1973b). An alternative method in the use of repertory grids. *Australian Psychologist, 8,* 213–219.

Rowe, D. (1976). Grid technique in the conversation between patient and therapist. In P. Slater (Ed.), *Explorations in intrapersonal space.* (Vol. 1). London: Wiley.

Rowe, D. & Slater, P. (1976). Studies of the psychiatrist's insight into the patient's inner world. In P. Slater (Ed.), *Explorations in Intrapersonal space* (Vol. 1). London: Wiley.

Rychlak, J. F. (1973). *Introduction to Personality and Psychotherapy.* Boston: Houghton Mifflin.

Ryle, A. (1975). *Frames and cages: The repertory grid approach to human understanding.* New York: International Universities Press.

Ryle, A. (1976). Some clinical applications of grid technique. In P. Slater (Ed.), *Explorations in intrapersonal space* (Vol. 1). London: Wiley.

Ryle, A. (1979a). Defining goals and assessing change in brief psychotherapy: A pilot study using target ratings and the dyad grid. *British Journal of Medical Psychology, 52,* 223–233.

Ryle, A. (1979b). Applications of repertory grid techniques. *Trends in Neurosciences, 2,* 46.

Ryle, A. (1982). A common language for the psychotherapies? In M. Goldfried (Ed.), *Converging themes in psychotherapy.* New York: Springer.

Ryle, A. & Breen, D. (1972a). A comparison of adjusted and maladjusted couples using the double dyad grid. *British Journal of Medical Psychology, 45,* 375–382.

Ryle, A. & Breen, D. (1972b). The use of the double dyad grid in the clinical setting. *British Journal of Medical Psychology, 45,* 383–389.

Ryle, A. & Lipshitz, S. (1974). Towards an informed countertransference: The possible contribution of repertory grid techniques. *British Journal of Medical Psychology, 45,* 219–225.

Ryle, A. & Lipshitz, S. (1975). Recording change in marital therapy with the reconstruction grid. *British Journal of Medical Psychology, 48,* 39–48.

Ryle, A. & Lipshitz, S. (1976a). Repertory grid elucidation of a difficult conjoint therapy. *British Journal of Medical Psychology, 49,* 281–285.

Ryle, A. & Lipshitz, S. (1976b). An intensive case-study of a therapeutic group. *British Journal of Psychiatry, 128,* 581–587.

Ryle, A. & Lunghi, M. E. (1969). The measurement of relevant change after psychotherapy: Use of repertory grid testing. *British Journal of Psychiatry, 115,* 1,297–1,304.

Ryle, A. & Lunghi, M. E. (1970). The dyad grid: A modification of repertory grid technique. *British Journal of Psychiatry, 117,* 323–327.

Ryle, A. & Lunghi, M. W. (1971). A therapist's prediction of a patient's grid. *British Journal of Psychiatry, 118,* 555–560.

Ryle, A. & Lunghi, M. W. (1972). Parental and sex-role identification of students measured with a repertory grid technique. *British Journal of Social and Clinical Psychology, 11,* 149–161.

Salmon, P. (1969). Differential conforming as a developmental process. *British Journal of Social and Clinical Psychology, 8,* 22–31.

Salmon, P. (1970). A psychology of personal growth. In D. Bannister (Ed.), *Perspectives in personal construct theory.* London: Academic.

Salmon, P. (1976). Grid measures with child subjects. In P. Slater (Ed.), *Explorations in intrapersonal space* (Vol. 1). London: Wiley.

Salmon, P. (January 1977). Developing our construing of developing social construing. *Forum: Journal of the British Psychological and Psychotherapy Association.*

Salmon, P. (1979). Children as social beings: A Kellyian view. In P. Stringer & D. Bannister (Eds.), *Constructs of sociality and individuality.* London: Academic.

Salmon, P., Bromley, J. & Presley, A. S. (1967). The word-in-context test as a measure of conceptualization in schizophrenics with and without thought disorder. *British Journal of Medical Psychology, 40,* 253–259.

Schuffel, W. & Schonecke, O. W. (1972). Assessment of hostility in the course of psychosomatic treatment of three patients with functional disorders: II. *Psychotherapy and Psychosomatics, 20,* 282–293.

Shapiro, C. A., Caplan, H. L., Rohde, P. D., & Watson, J. P. (1975). Personal questionnaire changes and their correlates in a psychotherapeutic group. *British Journal of Medical Psychology, 48,* 207–215.

Shaw, M. L. (Ed.). (1981). *Recent advances in personal construct technology.* London: Academic.

Sibilia, L., Liotti, G., Borgo, S. & Guidano, V. F. (1972). Analysis of reinforcement in the behavior of alcoholics by the use of Girglia's and Kelly's method. *Rivista di Psichiatria, 7,* 277–283.

Slater, P. (1960). The analysis of personal preferences. *British Journal of Statistical Psychology, 13.*

Slater, P. (1965). *The principal components of a repertory grid.* London: Vincent Andrews & Co.

Slater, P. (1969). Theory and technique of the repertory grid. *British Journal of Psychiatry, 115,* 1,287–1,296.

Slater, P. (1972). The measurement of consistency in repertory grids. *British Journal of Psychiatry, 121,* 45–51.

Slater, P. (Ed.). (1976). *Explorations of intrapersonal space, Vol. I: The measurement of intrapersonal space by grid technique.* London: Wiley.

Slater, P. (Ed.). (1977). *Dimensions of intrapersonal space, Vol. II: The measurement of intrapersonal space by grid technique.* London: Wiley.

Smail, D. J. (1972). A grid measure of empathy in a therapeutic group. *British Journal of Medical Psychology, 45,* 165.

Space, L. G. & Cromwell, R. L. (1978). Personal constructs among schizophrenic patients. In S. Schwart (Ed.), *Language and cognition in schizophrenia.* Hillsdale: Erlbaum.

Space, L. G., Dingemans, P. M. & Cromwell, R. L. (1982). Self-construing and alienation in depressives, schizophrenics, and normals. In J. R. Adams-Webber and J. Mancuso (Eds.), *Applications of personal construct theory.* Don Mills, Ontario: Academic.

Space, L. G. & Cromwell, R. L. (1980). Personal constructs among depressed patients. *Journal of Nervous and Mental Disease, 168,* 150–158.

Space, L. G. & Huntzinger, R. (1979). A micro computer-based psychopathology laboratory III: Hardware. *Behavior Research Methods and Instrumentation, 11,* 247–252.

Spelman, M. S., Harrison, A. W. & Mellsop, G. W. (1971). Grid test for schizophrenic thought disorder in acute and chronic schizophrenia. *Psychological Medicine, 1,* 234–238.

Stefan, C. (1977). Core structure theory and implications. In D. Bannister (Ed.), *New perspectives in personal construct theory.* London: Academic.

Stringer, P. (1970). Architecture, psychology: The game's the same. In D. Canter (Ed.), *Architectural Psychology.* London: RIBA publications.

Stringer, P. (1971). Some remarks on people's evaluation of environments. *Proceedings of the British Section of the Regional Science Association,* London.

Stringer, P. (1974). A use of repertory grid measures for evaluating map formats. *British Journal of Psychology, 65,* 23–34.

Stringer, P. (1975). The demands of personal construct theory. In G. Moore & G. Golledge (Eds.), *Environmental Knowing.* Strondsberg, Penn.: Dowden, Hutchinson & Ross.

Stringer, P. (1976). Repertory grids in the study of enviromental perception. In P. Slater (Ed.), *Explorations of intrapersonal space* (Vol. I). London: Wiley.

Stringer, P. (1979). Individuals, roles and persons. In P. Stringer & D. Bannister (Eds.), *Constructs of sociality and individuality.* London: Academic.

Stringer, P. & Bannister, D. (Eds.). (1979). *Constructs of sociality and individuality.* London: Wiley.

Sypher, H. E. & Applegate, J. L. (1982). Cognitive differentiation and verbal intelligence: Clarifying relationships. *Educational and Psychological Measurement, 42,* 537–543.

Takens, R. J. (1981). Commonality, sociality, and therapeutic accessibility. In H. Bonarius, R. Holland & S. Rosenberg (Eds.), *Personal construct psychology: Recent advances in theory and practice.* London: Macmillan.

ten Kate, H. (1981). A theoretical explication of Hinkle's implication theory. In H. Bonarius, R. Holland & S. Rosenberg (Eds.), *Personal construct psychology: Recent advances in theory and practice.* London: Macmillan.

Thomas, L. F. (1978). Learning and meaning. In F. Fransella (Ed.), *Personal construct psychology 1977.* New York: Academic.

Thomas, L. F. & Shaw, M. (1977). Pegasus: A manual. Centre for the Study of Human Learning, Brunel University, Uxbridge, England.

Thomas, L. F., Shaw, M. L., Beard, R., Pope, M. & Harri-Augstein, E. S. (1978). A personal construct approach to learning in education, training and therapy. In F. Fransella (Ed.), *Personal construct psychology 1977.* London: Academic.

Tyler, M. (1981). Kelly's "road to freedom"? In H. Bonarius, R. Holland & S. Rosenberg (Eds.), *Personal construct psychology: Recent advances in theory and practice.* London: Macmillan.

Ullman, L. P. (1970). On cognitions and behavior therapy. *Behavior Therapy, 1,* 201–204.

van den Berg, O., De Boeck, P. & Claeys, W. (1985). Schizophrenia. In E. Button (Ed.), *Personal construct theory and mental health.* London: Croom Helm.

Viney, L. L. (1980). *Transitions: Women experiencing change.* Sydney: Cassell.

Viney, L. L. (1984). Concerns about death among severely ill people. In F. R. Epting & R. A. Neimeyer (Eds.), *Personal meanings of death: Applications of personal construct theory to clinical practice.* New York: Hemisphere/McGraw-Hill.

Viney, L. L. & Westbrook, M. T. (1976). Cognitive anxiety: A method of content analysis for verbal samples. *Journal of Personality Assessment, 40,* 140–150.

Warr, P. B. (1971). Pollyanna's personal judgments. *European Journal of Social Psychology, 1,* 327–338.

Warr, P. B. & Coffman, T. L. (1970). Personality, involvement and extremity of judgment. *British Journal of Social and Clinical Psychology, 9,* 108–121.

Warr, P. B. & Jackson, P. (1977). Salience, importance and evaluation in judgments about people. *British Journal of Social and Clinical Psychology, 16,* 35–45.

Warren, N. (1964). A symposium on the theory and methodology of George Kelly. Unpublished proceedings, Brunel University, London.

Warren, N. (1966). Social class and construct systems: An examination of the cognitive structure of two social class groups. *British Journal of Social and Clinical Psychology*, 5, 254–263.

Warren, W. G. & Parry, G. (1981). Personal constructs and death: Some clinical refinements. In H. Bonarius, R. Holland & S. Rosenberg (Eds.), *Personal construct psychology: Recent advances in theory and practice.* London: Macmillan.

Watson, J. P. (1970). A repertory grid method of studying groups. *British Journal of Psychiatry*, 117, 309–318.

Watson, J. P. (1972). Possible measures of change during group psychotherapy. *British Journal of Medical Psychology*, 45, 71–77.

Wood, R. & Napthali, W. A. (1975). Assessment in the classroom: What do teachers look for? *Educational Studies*, 1, 151–161.

Wooster, A. D. (1970). Formation of stable and discrete concepts of personality by normal and mentally retarded boys. *British Journal of Mental Subnormality*, 16, 24–28.

Zelhart, P. & Jackson, T. T. (1983). George A. Kelly, 1931–1943: Environmental influence on a developing theorist. In J. R. Adams-Webber and J. C. Mancuso (Eds.), *Applications of Personal Construct Theory.* Don Mills, Ontario: Academic.

INDEX